D1119387

Life Moments for Women

100+ Extraordinary California Women Share a Turning Point in Their Lives

Patty DeDominic and Maureen Ford

ISBN 978-1-883423-27-8

First Edition
10 9 8 7 6 5 4 3 2 1

Cover & Book Design by Cathy Feldman
Book Production by Blue Point Books

Photography credits:
Page 3: Roclord Studio
Pages 105, 322, 323: Deb Halberstadt, Half City Productions
Page 176: Phillip Ritchie
Page 195: Piper Ferguson
Page 297: Terry Lorant

Profits from the sales of this book will go toward raising $1,000,000 for the Women's Foundation of California that supports California non-profits benefitting women and families.
www.womensfoundca.org

For more *Life Moments for Women* go to www.lifemomentsforwomen.com
To order this book in quantity for your organization please contact the publisher.

Published by
Blue Point Books
P.O. Box 91347
Santa Barbara, CA 93190-1347
800-858-1058
bpbooks@west.net • www.bluepointbooks.com

We dedicate this book to our extraordinary mothers

Mary Murphy Kohut

&

Eleanor Margaret Timm

who loved passionately and never stopped
encouraging our dreams.

Table of Contents

Introduction

As we work to create light for others, we naturally light our own way.

~ Mary Anne Radmacher

The day after I was named Publisher of the Los Angeles Times, a female co-worker stopped by my office. She said that her nine-year-old daughter had been coming to "Bring Our Daughters to Work Day" for the last couple of years and wanted to know if she could grow up to be Publisher of the paper. My co-worker didn't know how to respond until she read about my appointment. The young girl beamed when her mother showed her the story and said "Yes! You can grow up to be the Publisher!"

Throughout my life, I have learned from and been inspired and challenged by my family, friends and all the people I have worked with, worked for, and admired from afar. Many of the books that shaped my professional development included personal stories that expanded my understanding of life and success. Most of these stories were men's stories, powerful in extraordinary ways, yet sometimes alien to me as a young woman. I wish I could have read *Life Moments for Women* when I was in search of other women's experiences!

When Patty DeDominic and Maureen Ford called me with their idea for this book, I was thrilled. How amazing to have a collection of stories of crucible moments from successful women to inspire and motivate others who face their own challenges. I knew these two strong, courageous, talented and successful women would bring this book to fruition. And they have.

For the past eleven years, I have been a donor and board member of the Women's Foundation of California, a publicly supported grant-making foundation that invests in women as a key strategy for creating a California where all communities are economically secure and can thrive. I was overwhelmed with gratitude when Patty and Maureen generously decided to use the profits from this book to help raise $1,000,000 for the Foundation.

Since 1979, the Women's Foundation of California has cultivated and sustained diverse, trusted, cross-sector, cross-community relationships by making grants to effective community organizations, training nonprofit leaders, and bringing the voices of women into public policymaking. We focus on economic security because economic security is the key to building healthy, safe and flourishing communities.

Patty and Maureen's idea to use the incredibly compelling stories in *Life Moments for Women* as a fundraising tool for the Foundation and our grant partners is brilliant—as is their plan to replicate this model for nonprofits in other states across the nation. All of us at the Women's Foundation of California are deeply grateful to them and to all the courageous women who have shared a special moment in their personal life journey with us.

Kathryn Downing
Chair, Board of Directors
Women's Foundation of California

www.womensfoundca.org

Preface

Sooner or later we all discover that the important moments of life are not the advertised ones, not the birthdays, the graduations, the weddings, the great goals achieved. The real milestones are less prepossessing. They come to the door of memory unannounced, stray dogs that amble in ... and simply never leave. Our lives are measured by these.

~ Susan B. Anthony

We were strangers when we met for lunch on a beautiful spring day in Beverly Hills. How could we have known that moment was the start of a journey that would bring us into the hearts and souls of 100+ remarkable women across the state?

Timing, it is said, is everything. Patty DeDominic, entrepreneur, philanthropist, and women's advocate, had recently sold her award-winning staffing business. She had time to fulfill her vision of producing a series of Women's Festivals around the world to celebrate a very special day for all women.

In 1997 the United Nations General Assembly had proclaimed March 8 to be the official United Nations Day for Women's Rights and International Peace. The intent was to recognize the accomplishments of women throughout history and bring much-needed attention to the plight of millions of less fortunate women world-wide. Patty's goal was to create greater awareness of what is now known as International Women's Day.

Maureen Ford had just left her nineteen-year career as an entrepreneurship educator and was thinking about what to do next. She couldn't count the number of times her deeply inspired college students had said, "If you could find a way to bottle the life stories of the business leaders you have introduced us to, you could make a million dollars." She realized that while the business lessons in her program were of great academic value, the intimate sharing of personal experiences had changed her students' lives.

This is how the story of *Life Moments for Women* began—with the two strangers leaving that lunch as friends. Maureen joined Patty's host committee for the first International Women's Festival in Santa Barbara; Patty agreed to help Maureen find a way to "bottle" the "life-moments" of amazing women. The goal: to raise a million dollars for the Women's Foundation of California.

During the final year of working on this book, something bigger began to emerge. We were exploding with ideas and opportunities! Could *Life Moments for Women* be the birth of a movement - a movement of discovering within ourselves the pivotal turning points that shaped our lives—a movement of sharing these personal moments so that other women and girls can learn and grow from our unique life experiences? Not just in California, but around the country, maybe even the world!

Perhaps this book is the first step in that movement. The 100+ stories included here, many of them never before shared, prove that women everywhere share a common bond. It is our wish that *Life Moments for Women* will lead you toward a path to a better tomorrow.

Maureen Ford
Patty DeDominic

Life Moments for Women

Gisselle Acevedo

Making It Happen

Life is what we make it, always has been, always will be.

~ Grandma Moses, American folk artist

After fifteen hours of driving through a blinding snowstorm to get my daughter to an audition for admission into a college performing arts program, she breathed a giant sigh of relief when we arrived on time. Looking at her, I smiled and said, "Have you forgotten whose daughter you are?"

I am an immigrant, born in Costa Rica, and raised by a single parent. The first time my mother and I came to America, we landed in the South during the throes of the civil rights movement and racial segregation in the 1960's. I was six years old, and neither of us spoke a word of English. My mother's vision was to give me an education, something she never had. What happened next proved to be one of the most pivotal moments in my life.

After the airplane ride, I was hungry so we went to a small café and tried to order food. Suddenly, people started shouting and yelling at us in a language we couldn't understand. They called the police demanding that we be arrested. I clutched my mom in terror when they arrived and tried to take me away from her. My mother was unaware of the crime she had committed — sitting at a table on the "wrong" side of a racially segregated café.

We went back to Costa Rica thinking that maybe I couldn't receive a good education in this country after all. I still recall the fear that I experienced in that cafe, but I can only imagine how my mother felt as an immigrant Spanish-speaking woman trying to defend herself with a small child and no husband. I also remember thinking, "I will never allow myself to feel inferior. And I will never be yelled at or treated like this ever again."

I decided that whatever I was going to be, I would be somebody who could stand on her own two feet. Somehow my mother and I were going to make it. It was almost as if I saw my entire future knowing that everything I did from that moment on would move me toward success. Five years later we returned to America, this time to Los Angeles. My mother still had her vision of giving me an education.

She worked three or four low paying jobs at a time to make ends meet. For children living in poverty, the chances of getting a good education are very low. But the fortitude and tenacity of this determined woman defied those odds for me. Recently, when my mother, daughter and I were seated at a very elegant restaurant after my daughter's high school graduation, I turned to my mother and said, "You know, many years ago we were kicked out of a café, and now we are all here celebrating in this place because of you."

When you want something bad enough, you can do it. There is no excuse for not figuring out what your vision is and making it happen. Today my mother is eighty years old and is taking classes to get her high school degree.

~ Gisselle Acevedo

Gisselle Acevedo graduated with a Masters in Education and later received a law degree. After an illustrious career in media, public relations, law and education (including Vice President of Public Affairs for the Los Angeles Times and General Manager of Hoy, the Spanish language newspaper) she served as President & CEO of Para Los Ninos, a family services agency in Los Angeles for six years.

Aileen Adams

Taking a Stand

Women who survive harm or violation by another have power to send messages of hope, motivation and inspiration. Their painful experiences unveil true warriors, warriors who use their experiences as a tool to help others.

~ Rebecca Gray Grossman, Founder,
Grossman Burn Foundation

Thirty years ago, I met a courageous young woman who would change my life forever. A graduate student in library sciences, she happened to be the last passenger on a bus back to school from her job in downtown Los Angeles late one afternoon. Suddenly, the driver stopped the bus and parked in a very secluded location.

With his badge pinned to the lapel of his official uniform, he approached the student in a menacing way. She became so terrified that she experienced "frozen fright," a temporary response that can occur when the body "freezes" in response to a threat. The young woman was literally unable to scream or move when the driver began to undress her. After raping his terrified victim, the driver instructed her to redress and leave the bus. Three days later, she went to a local Rape Treatment Center and reported the crime.

At the time, I was a new lawyer volunteering at the center to help rape victims in need of legal assistance. My heart went out to this traumatized graduate student. When the director of the Rape Treatment Center and I contacted the District Attorney's office on the student's behalf, we were shocked to learn that the case could not be prosecuted because California law mandated that a rape victim forcibly resist her attacker.

To our horror, the bus company would not proceed against the driver either. Angry and outraged, we lobbied the company until they finally agreed to hold an administrative hearing. Upon listening to the young woman's compelling testimony, the bus driver was immediately dismissed from his job.

I had always known that rape victims were discriminated against. Traditionally, some sexual assault laws required an eyewitness to corroborate the crime. In many instances, victims were put on trial with their past sexual history used against them. I found it appalling to learn that California was one of twelve states that still required a woman to forcibly resist her attacker. Sometimes, resisting an attack can escalate violence.

We used this young woman's case to rewrite the California Sexual Assault Law, removing the victim resistance provision. My proudest moment was when the California Legislature passed our proposal in 1980, resulting in a new law that was heralded by the Los Angeles Times as one of the most important passed during that session. Thankfully, the California Supreme Court upheld the statute the following year.

Since then I have had many different jobs, including as a Cabinet Secretary for the State of California and Director of the

Office for Victims of Crime in the United States Justice Department. Now I serve as a Los Angeles Deputy Mayor. In each position, I have carried with me lessons learned from this case. The first is that victims should be at the center of the criminal justice system, instead of on the outside looking in. The second is that public policy, which benefits many, is often shaped by one courageous person who steps forward and takes a stand.

Being an effective public official means listening to and learning from the people we serve—shaping public policy based upon real life experiences. Very often, one person's violation can be used to change a law that will protect other people from similar crimes and abuses.

I don't know where this young woman is today, but every woman and man living in California has a lot to thank her for. She not only was instrumental in changing the state's rape law, her case is an example of the incalculable ripple effect that one courageous individual can have upon the lives of countless others.

~ Aileen Adams

Aileen Adams is the Deputy Mayor for Strategic Partnerships in Los Angeles. Previously, she served as Secretary for the State and Consumer Services Agency, a cabinet position in California. She also worked as a Presidential appointee in the U.S. Justice Department where she headed the Office for Victims of Crime—the top federal advocate for rights and services for crime victims. In addition, for many years, Aileen chaired the board of the Women's Foundation of California.

Kathie Armstrong

Magic in Sumba

A daughter is the happy memories of the past, the joyful moments of the present, and the hope and promise of the future.

~ Author Unknown

I glanced at my seventeen-year-old daughter with apprehension. Was I was doing the right thing taking her to a third world country with primitive tribal rituals, a jungle environment rife with malaria and dysentery? How would Abbie relate to indigenous natives who lived in grass huts without electricity, running water or toilets?

When we volunteered to work with other families in Sumba that summer, it seemed like a good idea, exciting, even glamorous, but now that we were on the plane preparing for takeoff, it was scary. Indonesia was rocked by a large earthquake earlier that day! The instant we set foot on the island, Abbie and I experienced a culture so foreign that it felt as if we had taken a gigantic step back in time.

I was astonished to see how quickly my daughter, the product of a sheltered and privileged environment, adjusted and thrived.

She threw herself enthusiastically into every available activity: painting murals in schools, playing soccer with the kids, distributing clothing and malaria nets in villages and dispensing discarded eyeglasses.

Abbie was most excited about her assignment working with the volunteer dentist, a job that entailed holding a "spit bucket" so villagers with infected teeth, rotted from chewing betel nut, could eject blood and mucus accumulated during extraction. I couldn't bear to watch and was relegated to sterilizing instruments. But my daughter graduated to pulling teeth by herself!

We noticed how many villagers waited patiently for their turn to be treated and had to come back day after day. Abbie decided that she wanted the money she had collected from a fundraising effort prior to our trip to go toward the training and education of a young Sumbanese nurse. However, we learned that most Sumbanese, if they go to school at all, usually don't progress beyond third grade.

The president of the Sumba Foundation said he had met thousands of villagers. Not one had ever left the bush for school. Motorbiking through a small village about an hour later, he came upon a celebration in progress—a young girl had just passed a test to attend nursing school in another town, but her parents didn't have the means to pay for it. As if by magic, the perfect candidate was found that day!

I'll never forget our gathering on bamboo mats outside a village hut. Abbie smiled at a shy olive-skinned girl named Margaretha as it was explained in Indonesian that the American teenager with the fair complexion and red hair would pay for three years of nursing school. I still get chills just thinking about it.

Margaretha was stunned! Her family jumped up to shake my hands and hugged and thanked Abbie. It's impossible to describe the depth of my emotions as I watched these two young women knowing that from that moment on they would always be connected.

Since Margaretha doesn't have a postal address, she and Abbie are only able to correspond when mail can be hand-delivered. Abbie's latest package contained a photograph of a proud young student nurse in a white uniform and a simple handwritten letter that began with "Hello my Sister ..." Abbie, who has been preparing for her own career in medicine, has recently received a grant to research malnutrition in Sumba!

I have always believed that doing your part to better the world would bring its own reward. Now I know that doing together it with someone you love is reward enough.

~ Kathie Armstrong

Kathie Armstrong is the founder of the Quiksilver Foundation, a nonprofit organization sponsored by Quiksilver, Inc., a multinational apparel and accessory company for youth. The Foundation is committed to benefiting and enhancing the quality of life for communities of surfers and board riders around the world with a special focus on children, education, science, oceans and the environment.

www.quiksilver.com

Tracy Austin Holt

Seeing the Big Picture

If you're a champion, you have to have it in your heart.

~ Chris Evert

Many people discover their passion later in life, but I was lucky to find mine at an early age. I feel fortunate to have grown up in a tennis-playing family of five brothers and sisters. Even at forty-eight, I still love the action, strategy and movement of a match, the exhilarating challenges of a tournament or just hitting the ball with my husband and sons.

I was sixteen and in pigtails in 1979 when I defeated reigning champion, twenty-four year old Chris Evert favored to win the U.S. Open title for the fifth consecutive year. I'll never forget the tension, the build-up, the excitement. Our styles of play were similar, and the match was so close. But I did it! I won 6-4, 6-3! I had reached the pinnacle of my sport, a goal I had been working toward for a long time.

Instantly famous, I didn't understand how winning the championship would change my life. I was recognized everywhere I went! My schedule became so busy and filled with commitments that it had to be professionally managed. Along the way, I learned about the importance of setting goals, the key to winning in all aspects of life.

Too often people set little goals and want to accomplish them quickly, but I believe that bigger goals are worth the wait. The larger the goal, the harder I work, and the sweeter the reward. Knowing that each step forward is a goal in itself is how athletes develop the champion attitude of persistence and mental toughness. We keep our minds focused on the end result and off the setbacks that get in our way.

A few years after winning my first U.S. Open, I was in New Jersey for a team tennis tournament. As I made a left turn driving away from my hotel, another driver ran a red light going 65 miles an hour and crashed into my side of the car. It wasn't until later, when I looked at photographs of the accident, that I realized how lucky I was to be alive.

Suddenly I saw the "big picture." The exhilaration and excitement of wining a championship title became so "little picture" when I realized that life can change in an instant. Sometimes things happen that are completely out of our control.

I began to appreciate the everyday moments with the people I love so much more. Keeping a positive attitude, I set a new goal and patiently and persistently worked through a year of intense physical therapy for my badly shattered leg. Plugging away day by day, I remained focused on the end result—getting back in the game again.

Don't let your life get so busy that you can only see the little picture. Once in a while, step back and think about what's really important. Focusing on the big picture will help to keep things in perspective and will enable you to tackle your personal challenges with strength and confidence.

~ Tracy Austin Holt

Tracy Austin Holt *is a former World Number One female professional tennis player who won the women's singles at the U.S. Open in 1979 and 1981 and the mixed doubles at Wimbledon in 1980. In 1992 she became the youngest person to be inducted in the International Tennis Hall of Fame. Tracy won thirty single titles during her years on the court. Today, in addition to being a full-time wife and mother to three sons, she serves as a commentator for the BBC and USA Network and the Tennis Channel.*

Karen Bass

Fighting for Justice

…We cannot afford to be separate …We have to see that all of us are in the same boat.

~ Dorothy Height, social activist

When I think about the many opportunities that women have today, I always remember two earth-shattering events that rocked my world when I was just fourteen.

Listening to the election results on the radio, I heard the devastating news that Bobby Kennedy had been assassinated. The shocking announcement, on the heels of Martin Luther King's assassination, stunned the nation and traumatized me. I had worked on his campaign! An African American teenager, I suddenly felt insecure and frightened. What would these two back-to-back, incomprehensible deaths mean for the future?

I had so much faith that these men could change the world but now they were gone! Suddenly, it seemed as if all my hopes and dreams for equality were disappearing too. At the same time, something stirred inside me. I wanted to make my own commitment to the battle for civil rights. That was the moment I decided what the focus of my life would be.

Growing up in the Venice-Fairfax section of Los Angeles, I understood the pain of racial discrimination. Many of my friends' parents would not permit their children to play with me. I wasn't invited into their homes; they weren't allowed into mine. The dual assassinations drove home the point that the racial divide was even more serious than I had realized—fighting for justice could mean the ultimate sacrifice of losing your life.

On a deeper level, I instinctively knew that one way of dealing with these devastating events was to try to turn such senseless tragedy into victory. If you get sad enough and mad enough, it is possible to focus your energy on constructive solutions and positive action. This awareness led to a set of core values that have shaped my life.

For me, that meant getting involved in politics and dedicating my time on earth to the battle for equality and justice. At the age of fourteen I mistakenly believed that one person could change the world. Now I know that it will take a movement of dedicated people working together to accomplish what no individual can do alone.

Not long ago, political and leadership opportunities for women were very rare. Today, every woman has the chance to be remembered as someone who made a difference.

~ Karen Bass

Karen Bass is the United States Representative for California's 33rd Congressional District. She made history when the California Assembly elected her to be its 67th Speaker catapulting her to become the first African American woman in the country and the first Democrat woman to serve in this powerful state legislative role.

Teri Bialosky

Making the Sale

The greatest disservice we can do for ourselves is to fail to appreciate who we already are ... Stop selling yourself short and you'll discover just how wonderful and fulfilling this life can be.

~ Noelle C. Nelson, Ph.D., author

Once, when speaking with a friend about what I wanted to do, he said, "There are three ways that a woman today can make really good money. You can become a professional like a doctor or a lawyer; you can start your own business—or you can go into sales."

Since I hadn't graduated college, the first choice wasn't an option. Starting a business was something that I didn't think I was capable of. As far as selling, the fear of rejection scared me to death. I was convinced that no one would ever buy anything from me. If someone were to turn me down, I would hide in a corner somewhere and cry.

I was working as an administrative assistant in a real estate company when I got up the nerve to try selling giftware. My first sale was with personalized pencils at a local drug store in Long Beach. "Hi," I said to the store manager nervously, "I'm Teri, and I'd like to check on the supply of my company's products." Noticing that certain pencils were out of stock, I asked if he would like to place an order. When he said, "YES!" I was so excited.

Selling was not only fun, it came naturally to me! Something that I feared and thought I could never do was actually an instinctive part of who I was. I couldn't wait to try again.

Years later, employed at a printing company in an outside sales position, I was consistently the top producer and the only working mom with young children at home. One weekend when I went to the office to catch up on paperwork, I discovered that everybody's desk had been cleaned out. The office was deserted! The rest of the sales force had abandoned the ship to start a rival organization and I wasn't invited to join them.

My first reaction was total shock; then I felt insulted, and finally I was extremely hurt. Why wouldn't my co-workers ask me, a proven sales person, to come along? I still don't know the answer. In retrospect, it was the best thing that could have happened because that was the genesis of my becoming an entrepreneur. Until that moment I was living inside my comfort zone and didn't see a need to rock the boat. But now I was ready to become captain of the ship and chart my own course.

I started to write a business plan, and nearly all of my former clients said that no matter what the plan looked like, they wanted to do business with me. They respected how I had treated them and appreciated the excellent customer service that I had always provided. Upon opening, my new company was in the black within 90 days, and soon I was earning more than I had as an employee.

This experience taught me that good relationships are everything no matter what your chosen field might be. How you treat other people, your customers, family and friends, and how they treat you is really all that matters at the end of the day.

I also learned that many women underestimate their instinctive capabilities and skills. When I finally stopped selling myself short and became the captain of my own ship, the real life-lesson of a career in sales finally sank in—no risk, no reward.

~ Teri Bialosky

Teri Bialosky is president and founder of Print Technology that provides both corporation communications and branded merchandise to a wide range of industries. She is a former president of the Los Angeles National Association of Women Business Owners and the Organization of Women Executives. Teri received the Women in Business Award from the Small Business Association and was inducted into the NAWBO-LA Hall of Fame.

www.print-technology.com

Karen Smith Bogart

A Competitive Advantage

Don't bury your natural feminine leadership strengths — flaunt them! Research has proven that a woman's inherent skills are beneficial to the health of a business: developing people, inspiring, empathizing, and big picture thinking, to name a few.

~ Katie Snapp, leadership trainer

I don't know if there will ever be a time when a capable business woman isn't judged by observable differences including her body shape and size, the clothes she wears, or the color of her skin. But I have learned that it is possible to open the minds of people who underestimate the value of smart and talented women.

When I started my career, nine times out of ten, I was the only female in critical business meetings. With an Undergraduate Degree in Political Science, a Masters in Industrial Relations, and an MBA, it was very frustrating to hear someone say "She's young and a woman—what does she know?" Over and over I thought, "Do I really have to prove myself … again!"

In the mid-1990s, as general manager and vice president for the camera division of a multinational imaging corporation, my business required many negotiations in Japan. In one meeting with four of my male co-workers and executives of a Japanese camera manufacturing company, I entered the board room and noticed that my team's business cards were laid out on the conference table in the traditional hierarchical way. It was assumed that as a woman I was a translator, so my card was on the bottom.

Here we go … again! After introductions were made and the Japanese executives learned that I was the key decision maker, cards were immediately rearranged, and mine was placed on top. During the meeting the executives continually showed surprise by my knowledge of the business operations which only served to increase my frustration of being repeatedly underestimated simply because of my gender.

Later that evening, according to Japanese custom everyone went to dinner. There was tremendous curiosity about my personal life including my marital status, my husband, children, and childcare arrangements. I was surprised and touched when one gentleman took me aside and said, "I really want to talk to my daughter about you. My wife didn't have options, but I want my daughter to know that she can do many things."

I realized that I was helping to pave the way for other young women! A female executive was a new role model for this man and his colleagues. I had been using my innate feminine leadership style—blending business knowledge and negotiation skills with friendliness, warmth, caring and humor, as a competitive advantage to turn skeptical assumptions about me upside down and open minds!

In that moment I let go of my frustration about having to constantly prove myself. I knew that I had served my company well and created the possibility that other women could follow in my wake. It confirmed my belief that competence always prevails in the end.

~ Karen Smith Bogart

***Karen Smith Bogart**, a proven global business manager, was Senior Vice President of Eastman Kodak Company and Chairwoman and President of Greater Asia located in China. Previously, she managed many of Kodak's largest global businesses each with revenues of $1B − $2.5B USD. She now is the President of Pacific Tributes, Inc., a business advisory firm focused on firm start-up, growth, and turn-around. Karen also serves on the Board of Directors of two public and one private US companies.*

Kay Buck

An Unexpected Search for Sisterhood

Help one another, is part of the religion of sisterhood.

~ Louisa May Alcott, American novelist

I was seven when my sixteen-year-old sister was killed by a drunk driver. Her tragic death turned my world upside down. My sister and I shared a bedroom and confided in each other. Suddenly, the big sister whom I looked up to and admired was gone forever. It felt as if there was an enormous hole in my heart that just got bigger as time went on. I never stopped yearning for the love, trust, and camaraderie that only a sister can give.

In retrospect, this yearning, coupled with the recognition of gender inequalities (yes, even a seven-year-old can see it!) drew me to work within a women's community. My career began in Asia as an advocate for survivors of sex slavery and human trafficking where I learned about the amazing resilience of the human spirit. The victims I supported had suffered heart-wrenching abuse, yet their resilience was palpable. I discovered, as they did, that when women are empowered together, our strength can overcome almost anything.

Returning to the West, I was certain about one thing: fighting for the freedom of women and girls was my life's work. After leading several initiatives to end violence against women in California, I had the honor of convening a community of human trafficking survivors—courageous women who are using their voices to develop strategies and solutions to stop modern-day slavery around the world.

A few years later I became pregnant for the first time. I found myself missing my sister more than ever. I hadn't told anyone, not even my parents that I was expecting before I left for a three day business trip. I wasn't showing, but I was physically sick and filled with fear about my ability to be a good mom.

At the airport, a familiar woman came up to me smiling and said, "I've been watching you. You're pregnant." Stunned, my immediate reaction was guilt. Flor, a survivor from a Los Angeles sweat shop, had suffered unspeakable violence at the hands of the trafficker. We were on our way to a conference where she would receive a medal of courage from the U.S. Ambassador to the Vatican, and it was my job to be strong for her. Suddenly, our roles were reversed.

"Don't worry," Flor continued. "I understand what you are going through. When I was pregnant, I felt the exact same way." We talked about what it was like to be a new mother and how my unborn daughter would change my life for the better. "Bearing a child," Flor said, "is an amazing gift to the world."

Flor and I had worked together on a number of projects, but this was the first time we opened our hearts and related to each other woman to woman. I wasn't alone. I had a special sister right in front of me—someone who would always be there when I needed help, as much as I would always be there for her.

That moment was the culmination of my years of working with survivors and women activists who support them. I realized that I have a community of sisters around the world, not biological ones, but real sisters who fill my life with strength and inspiration. In my unexpected search for sisterhood, it became clear that the bond all women share is really quite extraordinary.

~ Kay Buck

Kay Buck is the CEO of the Coalition to Abolish Slavery & Trafficking, a Los Angeles based human rights organization that is at the forefront of the movement to end modern day slavery. Previously, she was the Director of the Rape Prevention Resource Center for the California Coalition against Sexual Assault. A member of the California Attorney General's transition team on victim's rights, Kay was recognized as a Change Maker Dream Maker by the Women's Foundation of California.

www.castla.org

Diana Bull

Mission Accomplished!

If society will not admit of woman's free development, then society must be remodeled.

~ Elizabeth Blackwell, first female doctor in the US

At the age of twenty-two, I became a REALTOR. Eager for advancement and professional development, five years later I served as chapter president of the Santa Barbara Women's Council of REALTORS. I was keenly aware of a "good old boys network" that women had trouble cracking into. After becoming the fourth female President for the Santa Barbara Association of REALTORS, I appointed several women to key leadership positions.

Nearly twenty years later, serving on the California Association of REALTOR'S Strategic Planning and Finance Committee, there was serious discussion about reducing the Board of Directors from 700 members to less than 70. "Let's run this organization more like a corporation" was the thinking.

I grew concerned that many women would be bumped out of leadership opportunities and came up with an idea how to make sure that these changes would not keep women from rising to the top of our ranks. Knowing that the Treasurer chaired the committee and directed the agenda, I decided to run for the position. In the ninety-five year history of the organization, a woman had never held this office. This was one "glass ceiling" that needed to be broken!

The California State Chapter of the Women's Council of REAL-TORS gave $10,000 to fund my campaign. I won the election by 82% of the vote! When my term was up, I became the first woman from Santa Barbara to serve as the California Association of REALTOR'S President and the third female President. Until then there were only one or two token women appointed to the Executive Committee. I made sure we broke that "glass ceiling" by appointing many more women to serve on my Executive Committee. That culture remains today.

Eleven years later, my REALTOR-daughter was asked to serve on the Executive Committee. Perhaps if I had not passionately cared to advance women in leadership and had the courage to change the culture of the association by running for election, I might never have seen her on the raised stage—looking out at 700 directors and holding an important position of leadership. What a proud moment! Mission Accomplished!

~ Diana Bull

Diana Bull, *acknowledged in "Who's Who of American Women," won the Santa Barbara Boss of the Year Award and is a life-time member of the California Scholarship Foundation. She was named a Mentor/Business Leader by the Santa Barbara Hispanic Chamber of Commerce and "Top 50 Women in Business" by the Pacific Coast Business Times. Diana was honored to enter the National Association of REALTOR'S Hall of Fame and serves as the 2012 President of the Santa Barbara Chapter of NAWBO.*

www.dianabull.com

Tess Cacciatore

Will You Know My Name

I have an everyday religion that works for me. Love yourself first and everything else falls into line. You really have to love yourself to get anything done in this world.

~ Lucille Ball, actress

A swirling feeling came over me as I went through security at the Los Angeles International Airport. I was on my way to Des Moines, Iowa to help my brothers plan our father's funeral and felt very alone even though I was surrounded by a hustling flow of people. In a deep fog of sadness, I wondered how I would get through the next few days of burying my father. Only three months earlier I had buried my mom.

I was directed to a hallway that I had never been through before in my twenty-plus years of traveling in and out of LAX. Stepping onto the moving walkway, I looked around and not one person was in that hallway with me. Perhaps the unusual quiet is the reason why I had never noticed the sound of music inside the airport before.

What was that song? "Tears in Heaven!" Of course! It had to be a sign from my dad!

The words penetrated my heart and took my breath away. I knew then that the calling I had from years gone by as a singer would give my father a tribute and show gratitude for both my parents who had always supported my dreams even though they didn't always understand them. I would sing "Tears in Heaven" at my father's funeral.

My parents had a strange, but wonderful relationship. Married three times, to each other, they could turn a room of people into a party filled with love, or have everyone duck and cover if an argument was imminent. Mom and Dad were "Ricky and Lucy" to the fullest—the handsome dark Italian with Latin flair and shy side, and my blue-eyed, red-headed, silly-filled outgoing mother affectionately called "Lucy" throughout her life.

My mother's dream was for my name to be in lights on the marquee of a movie theater. I don't think she ever got over her disappointment that I gave up my acting career and had never become a famous Hollywood star. I loved my career in entertainment, but my path took a turn away from the spotlight. I became involved in producing and traveling the world to help children in developing countries for my nonprofit organization.

When it was time to sing at my father's funeral, I could barely feel my legs move as I walked toward the piano. One of my younger female cousins, beaming proudly, gave me the last ounce of courage to get out the first note of "Tears in Heaven."

Will you know my name, if I see you in Heaven? Will it be the same, when I see you in Heaven? I'll carry on. I must be strong ...

I was taken aback by the feeling of freedom that suddenly swept over me! All at once, everything became clear: it was time to follow my calling and stand on my own two feet. That no matter where my life took me or whether the path led to being in the spotlight or not, wasn't as important as having my name etched in the minds and hearts of children who will remember me as someone who did her best to make a change in the world.

This is the legacy that I am striving to build with my mother's and father's spirits by my side.

~ Tess Cacciatore

Tess Cacciatore, *an award-winning multi-media producer, named her production company CarLou Interactive Media & Publishing in loving memory of her parents Carolynn and Lou. She is the Founder of the World Trust Foundation to help mentor young people to create a sustainable future. Tess, who has traveled extensively around the world to help women and children, received the Medal of Excellence out of the United Nations in Geneva Switzerland for her work in the field of "Edu-tainment."*

www.carloumedia.com   *www.worldtrust.org*

Dianne Callister

From My Heart

*Do you know where you're going to? Do you like the things that life
is showing you? Where are you going to? Do you know?*

~ Diana Ross, lyrics, theme from *Mahogany*

Music has always been a big part of my life. I grew up playing the
piano, and when my children were small, I put them to bed playing
the harp. On the mornings they didn't want to get ready for school,
I would play my banjo to wake them up and get them going.

They laugh about it now saying, "Can you believe that mom put
us to sleep with a harp and woke us up with a banjo!" This was how
my children grew up, but I had no idea that my harp would eventually lead me back to the place where I was born.

The harp came into my life when I was pregnant with my fourth
child. My adoptive parents inherited the Irish harp and brought it to
our house thinking that one of the children might like to learn how
to play it. After my baby was born I took my oldest daughter to

music school for lessons. She didn't enjoy it, but I became very interested.

Learning to play the harp came naturally for me. Other than being Irish, I know very little about my family background, so I was fascinated to receive an Irish instrument that produced such beautiful sounds. Discovering that it had power to soothe my children, I began to wonder if I could provide comfort to other children and people in distress.

The teacher was impressed with my ability and started to book me for events such as parties and weddings that she was too busy to handle. But I really enjoyed using my skill to soothe children in the inner city and to comfort people on skid row or in safe houses for victims of domestic violence. Then one day I was invited to play my harp at a Mother's Day luncheon at a Salvation Army Hospital in East Los Angeles.

The name of the hospital rang a bell. At first I didn't know why—and then I realized that I had seen it on my birth certificate. I went to check, and sure enough, I was going to play my harp at the exact same place where I was born and given up for adoption. I had never met my birth mother or knew anything about her. It was too difficult a topic to think about, and while my adoptive mother was alive, I felt it would be disloyal because she had always given so much of her heart and soul to raising me.

When I arrived at the hospital, I quickly noted the dismal surroundings. Transporting my harp through the dim hallways with bars on every window, I was humbled to retrace the steps taken by my birth mother almost fifty years earlier. I couldn't help but think about all the opportunities I had been given. I had grown up less than twenty miles away, but it was worlds apart from this sad place.

Perhaps it was the contrast between all the blessings I had been given and the wonderful life I led that made it such an intense emotional experience. It was the first time I ever fully understood the complete distress my birth mother must have felt walking down this hallway when she was pregnant with me.

Although I'll never know for sure, I imagined that my coming to being on this earth was probably the beginning of a really hard life for my birth mother. An array of feelings, including gratitude that I even existed at all, rushed over me. Seeing the frightened looks on the faces of the unwed mothers made me hope that I didn't destroy my birth mother's life because of the choice she made.

After I finished playing, a group of pregnant teenagers gathered around and wanted to know about my harp. They had never seen sheet music before and couldn't believe I was reading notes from a page. "Wow," I thought. "What very different worlds we live in." One of the girls asked, "Why are you here today? Are you getting paid?" Tapping his chest, the hospital director explained that I was a volunteer and was there because it came from my heart.

No one knew that I had been born there, and I wasn't sure if it was appropriate to tell them. All the girls left except for one who stayed behind. She looked very pregnant and I asked when she was due. She said, "I'm twice as unlucky as the others. I am pregnant with twins." Looking into her downcast eyes I replied, "Do you want to know a secret? I was born here, and if there is one thing I know for sure, it's that I'll always be grateful for having a mother like you. Something positive can come of this, wait and see."

Giving her a tearful hug, I heard her say, "Good-by, Angel." The moment was an awakening because I realized where I came from is not as important as where I am going. I can never go backwards and change my beginning. I can only go forward and create a happy ending. Each of us can do that, no matter what the circumstances of our birth—and no matter what our choices might have been along the way.

~ Dianne Callister

***Dianne Callister** is the president of the Singer Foundation that is dedicated to children and the challenges they face including poverty and hunger. She founded Project Give, a student-driven service project for middle schools across the country empowering students to become actively involved in identifying and solving problems in their local community. Dianne was honored as the 2010 National Mother of the Year.*

www.project-give.org

Karen Caplan

A Watershed Moment

Some are kissing mothers and some are scolding mothers, but it's love all the same.

~ Pearl Buck, author, Nobel Prize winner

I am the first-born daughter of entrepreneur, Frieda Caplan, and when it came to my mother, I grew up with a chip on my shoulder. From my perspective, she was never there for me as a parent. Work always came first. We only talked about business and never did any fun mother-daughter things like having lunch together or going shopping for clothes.

From the time I was fourteen years old, vacations and weekends were spent working at my mother's side at her stand in the Los Angeles Produce Market. She never encouraged or discouraged me to join the business, but when I suddenly announced as a sophomore in college that I wanted to make the produce industry my career, my mother was thrilled.

Frieda Caplan, the toughest business woman I have ever known, is a firm believer in starting at the bottom—literally. One of my earliest assignments was in the refrigerated section of the basement in our building taking inventory of fresh produce.

During the summer I had to be on the job at 2:00 am. Once I overslept and arrived at 4:45 am. After putting in a twelve-hour day, my mother called me into her office and said, "I noticed that you came in late today. You will be treated like everyone else. The next time you are late, I will fire you."

Having inherited my mother's passion for the produce business, I was never late again. But as hard as I tried to prove myself, I always felt like I was living in "Frieda's" shadow. Eventually, I worked my way into customer relations and then into sales, which came very naturally to me. Slowly I was coming into my own.

In 1986, I became president & CEO of the specialty produce business my entrepreneur-mother had started twenty-five years earlier. Still, my mother and I were never close. Then members of my CEO Forum convinced me to attend a powerful three-day personal development program that promised to dramatically improve the quality of my life.

On the last day of the course, each participant had to choose someone in their lives, an important person, they had a problem relating to. The person I chose was, naturally, my mother. What happened next was the most difficult thing I have ever had to do in my entire life—and it was also the most transforming.

The goal was to learn to accept my mother for who she was, not who I wanted her to be. Oh my God! I had to leave the class, go to a telephone, call my mother and say, "Hello Mom, this is Karen. I want to let you know that you are the perfect mother for me." Then I had to list all the reasons why.

I was so nervous! This was the last thing on earth I wanted to do. I remember going through this very emotional experience of feeling completely vulnerable and being totally open and honest with myself. The truth was that my mom is absolutely the perfect mother for me because if she wasn't who she was I wouldn't be who I am now.

My life was totally transformed when I accepted how great my mother really is. Suddenly, I began to appreciate things about her that used to bother me. I went through a complete metamorphosis and actually admired her for overcoming the challenges of starting a business in a male-dominated field during a time when most other women didn't work outside the home.

Since that watershed moment I have grown into a better and much happier person. Relationships with other people in my life became more meaningful. My self-esteem and confidence improved as I evolved into a more compassionate and tolerant daughter, mother, sister, boss, co-worker and friend.

Recently, my mom and I shared a very emotional conversation about my grandmother on the forty-ninth anniversary of her death. "You know, Karen," she said wistfully, "your grandmother was the sweetest, kindest, nicest person in the world. She never had a bad word to say about anyone." It struck me how my mother didn't see that she is that same sweet, kind and nice person—someone I'm always striving to be.

Decide to accept your parents, family and friends. Embrace them for the imperfect human beings that all of us are. No one is perfect. Never underestimate the transformative power of a positive relationship to increase your confidence and fill your life with joy.

~ Karen Caplan

***Karen Caplan** is President & CEO of Frieda's Inc, Past-Chairman of the Board of the United Fresh Produce Association (the first woman chair in 99 years), and a past Director of the Federal Reserve Bank in Los Angeles. She propelled Frieda's Inc. to the forefront of the produce industry as the nation's leading marketer and distributor of specialty produce. Karen, mother of two daughters, serves on a number of boards of directors and has received countless awards in business and for leadership roles in the community.*

www.friedas.com

Kim Carter

A Beacon of Light

I had crossed the line. I was free; but there was no one to welcome me to the land of freedom. I was a stranger in a strange land.

~ Harriet Tubman, African American
slave & abolitionist

My name is Kim Carter, and I was recycled in and out of prison for an addiction to crack cocaine. For twenty years I succumbed to the belief that incarceration was my fate and accepted the losing card that I thought I had been dealt.

My mother was a single parent of four, and I didn't know my dad. Everything I knew about drugs, alcohol, sex, and abuse, I learned in my home. Looking for love in all the wrong places, I became a promiscuous teenager and turned to drugs. Society responded to my destructive lifestyle by sending me to prison.

One day I learned about a pilot program to help drug addicted women in the California prison system. It was the first time I had ever heard the word "hope" in jail. There was a lot of excitement, but there were only 100 spaces for the 3,000 women who needed the help. They were looking for the worst cases of inmates who had been recycling in and out. I prayed that I would be one of the women called.

When they said that I was "Number 87," I couldn't believe that I had been chosen! During the program I was forced to confront all of the terrible things that had happened in my past, including childhood abuse, molestations and rape.

Recidivism and addiction is what I had accepted as my truth, but in reality it was not my truth. I learned that I wasn't a bad person; I was a sick person. I didn't know there was a cure for my illness. I also realized there were caring people who understood my disease, people who weren't like anyone I had met before. I began to heal unaware that I was on a path to freedom and would never use drugs or be sent to prison again.

Today I stand eighteen years later, a sober community activist and leader. I am convinced that I would still be in prison if I did not have access to treatment. I feel very blessed to have been given a new lease on life but wish that I had gotten this opportunity sooner.

I remember moving into my first apartment after rehab and, as I looked back at the past two years, I was surprised at how much I had grown and blossomed in such a short amount of time. During this transition I had to cut ties with close friends and some family members. I was no longer the same person who would go back to doing what she'd always done. I realized that no one would be there to welcome me to the new path I had chosen: a life free from drugs and incarceration.

I thought about the thousands of other incarcerated women who didn't know there was a way out. Maybe I could be their beacon of light! Maybe my journey to freedom could be an example to help them find their own path to freedom. In that moment it became clear that the next chapter of my life would be about lighting a path to let others know there is a way out.

~ Kim Carter

Kim Carter is the Founder and Executive Director of Time for Change Foundation that provides resources, programs and services to women and children who desire to change the course of their lives by making the transition from homelessness and recidivism to self-sufficiency. Kim is the recipient of multiple honors including the San Bernardino County's Humanitarian Award and the, Inland Empire Woman of Distinction Award. She is also an author and motivational speaker.

www.timeforchangefoundation.org

Jacqueline Caster

A Small Window of Time

To a father growing old nothing is dearer than a daughter.

~ Euripides

One day I'd like to write a book about the whole experience I had with my dad. The title would be "The Window" because as an adult that is what I had with my father—a small window of about a year before losing him to rapidly advancing dementia. Until then, we hadn't seen or spoken to each other in exactly twenty years.

It all started with a phone call from my father's cousin. "I'm worried about your dad," she said. "I can't reach him, and when I call his wife, she won't put him on the phone. Something is very wrong."

I didn't know how to respond, and I really did not want to get involved. My father had abandoned my mom for a younger woman and had completely severed contact with me and my siblings at the insistence of his new wife. He was practically a stranger! Still, I promised to call some of his old friends and see what I could discover.

I was astonished to learn that my father, a doctor, was in the early stages of dementia and had been forced by his partners to give up his fifty-year medical practice. He was being sequestered and seriously neglected by his vengeful wife. A classic case of elder abuse, my father's life was actually in danger!

My brother and sister refused to take any action on his behalf, but I decided to push past my feelings of betrayal and alienation. Making a flurry of arrangements, I hired attorneys and flew to Kansas City where my father was living. It wasn't exactly a "thought" that propelled me to reach out and help a parent in need; it was almost as if there was a force beyond my control encouraging me to do the right thing.

When I emerged from the rental car in my father's driveway, a tired old man stood on the doorstep. The once very dapper and nationally prominent doctor was a disheveled and disoriented mess. But he recognized me! All at once, mutual tears started to flow. I was still his daughter! He was still my dad! In that moment I knew that even after so many years and so much pain, our father-daughter connection was still intact.

Dad was eventually transferred to a nursing home, but not before the two of us had a chance to mend fences and catch up on the two decades we missed together. Five years later, unable to walk, talk or feed himself, he is now in a daze most of the time. We hold hands and I stroke his head so, in our own way, we are still connecting. Sometimes our eyes do meet, but for the most part, he is gone.

The memory of the small window of time that I had before losing my father forever reminds me of the joy that comes from helping others when no one else is willing to intervene.

~ Jacqueline Caster

Jacqueline Caster is a tireless advocate for disenfranchised youth. She is the Founder and President of the Everychild Foundation, a woman's philanthropy whose mission is to ease suffering of children in the Greater Los Angeles area whether due to disease, disability, abuse, neglect or poverty. A former attorney and city planner, she is often speaks nationally on the issues of juvenile justice reform and youth aging out of foster care. Jacqueline also serves on the board of the Washington D.C. based Campaign for Youth Justice.

www.everychildfoundation.org

Laura Chick

Hitting My Stride

You gain strength, courage and confidence by every experience in which you really stop to look fear in the face ... You must do the thing you think you cannot do.

~ Eleanor Roosevelt

Something inside me just snapped when my husband said, "Laura, there's no way. What you're thinking about is not done in politics. You can't do it."

For me to be able to say out loud, at a vulnerable point in my life, that I thought I could do this, and wanted to do this—only to be told that I can't—was the straw that broke the camel's back. So I became more determined than ever to do what my husband said was impossible: run for office and unseat my former boss, a 16-year incumbent.

To be fair, my husband's remark wasn't totally responsible for my sudden "snap." For as long as I could remember, I had been saying "no" to myself as well. Hadn't life also presented me with series of "no's" which, while trying to please others, I accepted? Now was the time to stand up for myself and say "yes" to Laura.

That is why, in the heat of the moment, I gave myself permission to do a few things that I would never have even considered before—like stepping forward in an unusually gutsy way, running for public office without any real experience, taking on a 16-year incumbent and breaking an "unspoken rule." Most of all, I risked having to hear the dreaded words, "I told you so."

Instead of encouragement, my family and friends wanted to know what was wrong with me. Their skepticism fell on deaf ears. I was not going to live the rest of my life based on other people's expectations of me—who I "should" be and what I "should" do, even if it meant being "politically incorrect."

Going back to graduate school in my early forties helped me to grow into my own skin and put me back in touch with a level of confidence and skills that I had forgotten I had since high school. The positive affirmation and validation of earning a master's degree at this stage in my life made me feel like I could succeed in anything. Most of all, I learned that the only opinion of me that really mattered was my own.

My intent was to walk the traditional path by becoming a clinical social worker, but I eventually realized that I didn't have the right personality for the job. Then another opportunity fell into my lap and shifted my career in a different direction.

When a Los Angeles City Councilwoman offered me a job, I wasn't sure this was something I wanted to do. Debating it in my head, I felt pulled toward the position. Something inside me started to say that my real calling was community work and being out in the field.

I accepted the offer but after a few years I started to think that I could handle my boss' responsibilities better and accomplish much more. Disillusioned with what I felt was her lack of energy and focus, I quit my job. As the next election approached, I felt the same "pull" telling me to step forward. My gut instinct said "Go girl!" and I answered the call.

I still remember being scared to death and feeling nauseous when I had to debate my opponents or give a speech. I was afraid of losing the election horrifically, making a fool of myself and embarrassing my family. My fears were unwarranted. I won the election and celebrated at my victory party dancing all night.

After the elation of winning wore off, reality set in. I felt overwhelmed by the huge responsibilities of public office. Was I really qualified to do this job? It took about six months before I could catch my breath and feel comfortable in my new role on the city council. Little did I know it was only the calm before the storm!

The epicenter of the catastrophic Northridge earthquake that struck California a few weeks later was directly below my council district. The home I was living in at the time suffered severe damage and we had to move out for many months while it was being repaired. This was a true test of my leadership ability and commitment to serve the community that I dearly loved. This disaster destroyed my property and possessions, but not my spirit.

After almost four weeks of working round-the-clock, I walked through the various tent cities that were set up to house people in local parks. I felt fortunate to have a job in politics where I could play out all my abilities and make a difference. I was hitting my stride! Proudly, I knew it was the right decision when, in the heat of the moment, I trusted my instincts enough to believe that I could do what couldn't possibly be done.

If you are passionate about something, don't listen to anyone who says you can't do it. Give yourself permission to succeed. Say "Yes, I can!" and then, in a very strategic and thoughtful way, figure out how to make it happen.

~ Laura N. Chick

Laura N. Chick *has been a transformational and inspirational political leader. As a Los Angeles City Councilmember, Los Angeles City Controller and California Inspector General overseeing stimulus spending, she was a truth teller who took the job as the taxpayer's watchdog to an art form. Her constant battle against the status quo, waste and inefficiency struck a chord with the public and advanced responsible solutions to long standing problems.*

Jane Choi

Spreading My Wings

In helping others, we shall help ourselves, for whatever good we give out completes the circle and comes back to us.

~ Flora Edwards

At the age of thirteen, all I wanted was to be with my friends, so I was very unhappy when my parents announced that we were leaving Seoul, South Korea for America. "We want you to fly as high as you can," my mother consoled me. "We want you to spread your wings." It didn't take very long to fall in love with my new country and to appreciate the many opportunities that America afforded me.

After graduating college, I enjoyed my different positions in human resources, teaching, banking, and as a small business owner, but eventually I found myself longing for a career where I could make a positive impact on my community and grow professionally. As fate would have it, I was offered a job with New York Life Insurance Company.

Excited and ready for a new challenge, I joined the Kentucky office as an agent where two-and-a-half years later, I was promoted to Partner. My co-workers were very surprised when they learned that I had agreed to join the management team. Why would I want all the pressure and responsibility of being a manager when I was already successful and making a lot of money as an agent?

It was an important question, and one that I had to ask myself. Why did I want to be a manager? The answer that I came up with was that as an agent, I could build my own castle, but as a manager, I could build a city! My heart just said that becoming a manager was the right thing to do.

Sadly, three years later my mother became ill, and while I was visiting her in California, I received a call from one of my agents in Kentucky. The agent had worked hard for a year to close an important policy that was going to help a man establish financial protection and a legacy for his wife, children and grandchildren. At the last minute, the man suddenly cancelled, and the agent didn't understand why. She was very concerned that his family would be left with no financial protection if he suddenly died. Without the new policy, all his employees could be affected as well.

I felt torn. My mother was ill. At the same time this distraught young woman needed my support to help her make sure that the man's family and employees would be protected should something unexpected happen. It was more than just leaving a legacy; the lives of people were at stake. I knew what my mother would want me to do.

I flew to Kentucky where I worked with my agent and her client to explore all the legal and tax issues and to prepare a customized estate plan that the man really wanted. Then totally exhausted, I took the next flight back to California to be at my mother's side.

A few weeks later my mother passed away. After attending her funeral, I returned to my office in Kentucky where my agent was waiting for me with a beautiful bouquet of flowers. "Thank you so much," she said. "You helped save my client's family and his employees. They all are grateful to you. And so is my family. Your support has enabled me to move my own family into our first home."

The joy on my agent's face is something I will never forget. This was why I wanted to be a manager—to build a city and to nurture my people! To help them soar to their highest potential and achieve their dreams! To me, mentoring people and watching them spread their wings is the greatest reward of being a manager. My agent's success was my success!

I was filled with the profound sadness of losing my mother as well as the joy of knowing that I had made a positive impact on another family's life. Heartfelt words spoken long ago came back to me. "We want you to fly as high as you can. We want you to spread your wings." My parents came to America dreaming their daughter would lead a successful life, and in that moment I felt as if their dream had come true.

~ Jane Choi

Jane Choi is the Managing Partner of the Central Coast office of New York Life Insurance Company which is recognized as one of America's Most Admired Companies. Jane has won numerous national trophies and awards for her work with New York Life which led to becoming the first female member of the Managing Partner's Action Committee. She is proud to manage 50+ agents and Financial Service Professionals in Ventura, Santa Barbara County and San Luis Obispo.

www.centralcoast.nyloffices.com

Gillian Christie

On Top of the World

Running is like celebrating your soul. There's so much it can teach us in life.

~ Molly Barker, founder, Girls on the Run

Running has always been one of my greatest passions. As often as I can, I head for the hills near my home for an eight-mile round trip journey to the top of my favorite mountain. It's impossible to describe the glorious sense of freedom and elation that I feel traversing the peaks and valleys of this gorgeous terrain.

One day an adorable little dog suddenly appeared out of nowhere and adopted me as his running partner. When we reached the top of the mountain, I sat down on a rock and the little dog jumped up into my lap. There I was, sitting on top of the world, enjoying a magnificent view of the Pacific Ocean and the Santa Barbara Islands, cuddling my furry new friend, thinking, "Is this a glorious planet, or what?"

I thought about how, training for a triathlon a few years earlier, I had tripped on a rock running down a ravine slope, not far from where I sat, horribly twisting my leg in the wrong direction. My frantic screams for help went unheard until two hours later a hiker saw me dragging myself down the mountain in excruciating pain and called paramedics.

After three hours of surgery at a nearby hospital, I learned that I had broken my thigh bone and shattered my pelvis. When the doctor said that it would take a miracle to fully recover from the accident and I would most likely never run again, I was determined to prove him wrong. Never say never to me! Still, the independent life that I had always taken for granted was gone in an instant.

Confined to a wheelchair, it was humbling to rely on other people for my basic needs. Until then, full of adventure and freedom, I had always lived outside my body believing that I could just fly through life unscathed and untouched. The seriousness of my injuries made me understand that I needed to be more cautious and grounded in my thinking, to walk and run more slowly, and to learn how to combine my innate spirit of adventure with the skills of objective observation.

My disability also taught me to be a more compassionate and caring human being. I've always believed everything happens for a reason. Before my accident, I was only able to consider someone else's problems from an intellectual point of view, but in my wheelchair I could feel their pain deeply and personally.

The healing power of listening, really and truly listening, took me by surprise. It was amazing how I was able to lessen another person's suffering just by giving them my full and undivided attention—and how, in the same way, they could help to lessen mine.

Heading down the mountain with my running partner at my heels, I reminded myself to slow down and appreciate the journey more deeply. I reflected upon the peaks and valleys of my life and marveled at how everything is connected in the physical world in ways we'll never understand. In that moment, the only thing I knew for sure is this: with faith, persistence and sheer determination, a miracle can happen.

~ Gillian Christie

Gillian Christie is the founder and CEO of Christie Communications, an international public relations, marketing, and advertising agency offering custom-tailored marketing and public relations strategies for businesses, entrepreneurs and organizations making a difference. Gillian sits on the boards of Citizens for a Balanced Community and Safe Harbor, a nonprofit organization for Alternative Mental Heath. She is active in many other organizations including the Citizens' Commission on Human Rights.

www.christiecomm.com

Carla Christofferson   *Kathy Goodman*

A Positive-Sum Game

My guiding principle is that prosperity can be shared. We can create wealth together. The global economy is not a zero-sum game.

~ Julia Gillard, Prime Minister of Australia

We believe that the Los Angeles Sparks are the best female basketball players in the world! We also believe in everything this team represents—strong, powerful, inspiring women who perform at the highest level in their chosen profession for the love of the game. In today's world of sports, female basketball players don't do it for the money.

Long-time fans, we were at a game sharing opinions about how to promote the Sparks in a better way than was being done. How could these amazing athletes get the recognition they deserve? Suddenly, we looked at each other and said: "We should buy the team!"

We joked about our crazy idea until we realized that what was keeping us from buying the Sparks was the fact that no one expected us to do it. When we stopped asking "Why us?" and started saying "Why not us!" we got out of our own way and went for it.

Besides wanting to promote women in sports, our decision was based on the belief that we were getting in on the ground floor of an entrepreneurial opportunity. We also shared a vision: to present the players as positive role-models and help to change the culture by imparting the values we see on the basketball court into the community.

One way sports teams gain profitability is through corporate sponsorships. Convinced that the WNBA was a great brand match, we were excited when a well-known pharmaceutical company bought a large block of tickets to donate to seriously ill children and their families. We agreed to give the kids autograph coupons for players to sign.

The Sparks didn't win the game, but autographs still needed to be signed. The first child on line was a little girl in a wheelchair that her parents were struggling to get out of the stands and onto the court. All at once, the players took notice. They walked over to the child, knelt at her side, and showered the little girl with all their attention.

Everyone who saw what was happening got choked up with emotion. The parents looked on in tears, but the look on their daughter's beaming face said it all. She was grinning from ear-to-ear! Her eyes, wide like giant saucers and filled with excitement, seemed to say: "Is this really happening? Is this really happening to me?"

We were so proud of our players for immediately recognizing what needed to be done. But later as we processed what had occurred, we realized this was the intersection of everything we believed in. It is possible to connect the business side and the community side in a positive way.

When we became co-owners of the Sparks, many people said we would need to make a choice, that if we were looking at this as a philanthropic venture, we should just forget about the business side. We didn't believe them then, and we don't believe them now.

In retrospect, it was a positive-sum game. Everyone won! The pharmaceutical company gained respect and appreciation from the community they served; many children and their parents enjoyed a professional basketball game for the first time; we sold a lot of tickets, and our team shined as the outstanding role-model that we always knew they were.

Maybe the Sparks didn't win the game that night, but they transformed a little girl's life. It was an emotion-filled moment that we'll never forget. Life is not a zero-sum game where someone has to lose so that somebody else can win

~ Carla Christofferson & Kathy Goodman

Carla Christofferson is the managing partner of O'Melveny & Myers Los Angeles office and a member of the Business Trial and Litigation Practice. She was recognized as a Southern California "Super Lawyer" and named one of the Daily Journal's top 75 women litigators in California. Carla has received many honors including of the Women's Foundation of California Trailblazer Award, the Junior League Women in Leadership Award, and the Urban Economic Summit Living History Award.

www.omm.com

Katherine Goodman teaches high school English and Social Studies at High-Tech LA, an independent charter school in the San Fernando Valley. Prior to teaching, she served as President, West Coast Operations, of Intermedia Films. Kathy is a member of the Leadership Council of the Posse Foundation which supports college students through scholarships and peer support groups. In 2006 she formed Gemini Basketball LLC with Carla Christofferson to acquire the WNBA franchise Los Angeles Sparks.

Dallas Clark

The Day the Sun Came Out

I left my heart in San Francisco, high on a hill it calls to me, To be where little cable cars climb half-way to the stars! The morning fog may chill the air, I don't care!… Among the blue and windy sea … Your golden sun will shine for me!

~ Lyrics to *I left My Heart in San Francisco*

A small town, New Braunfels, Texas was my place of birth. By the mid-1950's I was a registered nurse working at M.D. Anderson Medical Center in Houston, Texas, when a friend asked me to accompany her on a visit to her aunt in California. Excited to see the Golden State, I said yes, packed my bags and we drove 1,700 miles to San Francisco.

Shortly after we arrived, a friend arranged a blind date, a very nice man who agreed to show me around town. The entire city was covered by a blanket of fog! Three days later, the fog magically disappeared. What a surprise! San Francisco was not only beautiful; it was spectacular with an incredible view around every corner.

As it turned out, I didn't fall in love with my date, but I did fall in love with San Francisco. I loved the remarkable California weather, the breath-taking terrain and the rich ethnic diversity of its people so much that I made what was a life-changing decision: to leave my nursing job in Houston and make San Francisco my home.

Although I had chosen a new life, I missed my close circle of friends and family including eight brothers and sisters more than I could have imagined. One day, overwhelmed with loneliness, I walked to a seaside cliff near my apartment and cried my heart out. All at once my attention was diverted by the sound of crashing waves.

I was standing on a bluff overlooking the majestic Pacific Ocean! There was so much natural beauty here! This was why I moved to San Francisco! That was the moment I knew California would always be my home, even though I had absolutely no idea what my future would bring.

Soon I found a job as a representative for a large national medical company promoting their products in seven western states, a big change for a small-town Houston girl like me. Suddenly, I was experiencing new things and expanding my horizons, meeting new people, speaking in front of groups, and traveling to many different places.

Looking back, so many wonderful things would not have happened in my life if I hadn't summoned the courage to take that enormous risk—leaving my familiar and safe environment and creating a new beginning in my beautiful city by the bay.

~ Dallas Clark

***Dallas Clark** and her first husband managed a company that served 125 hospitals and became involved in real estate investment partnerships that continue to this day. After moving to Santa Barbara with her second husband, they owned and operated the popular restaurant, Andria's Harborside Restaurant for ten years and produced several Santa Barbara International Jazz Festivals. Today, Dallas enjoys travelling with her composer/pianist/artist husband when he performs internationally.*

Vivian Clecak

Finding My Voice

Voices unheard ...it is not possible to estimate this great waste of talent, of potential!

~ Doris Lessing, Nobel Laureate

I was a graduate student at U.C.L.A. the day I lost my voice in class. When I opened my mouth and tried to speak, no sound came out at all. Overwhelmed by the realization that I literally could not talk, I hid my hands under the table so the other students couldn't see how badly they were shaking.

Although I had the ability to excel academically, I suffered from a painful feeling of shyness. It was easy to perform well on papers and tests but impossible to speak up and let my inner light shine after school or in social situations. In high school, if I saw a boy that I liked, I would quickly look the other way, terrified that if we made eye contact, he might not say hello. I would die of embarrassment! Literally and figuratively, I could not speak up or walk toward what I wanted most.

Because I was an excellent student, I went to college with the help of a full scholarship and arrived at Stanford University scared, lonely and only comfortable with a few close friends. When I graduated Stanford cum laude, I had gained poise and confidence but was still a very shy young woman.

During high school and as an undergraduate, I raised my hand and waited for permission to answer a question. But this was not the case in graduate school where controversial topics and exciting ideas were flying back and forth. The voices of my classmates were emotional, loud and intense. In order for me to take part in the discussion, I had to jump in and claim the right to be heard.

Filled with passionate thoughts about the many significant political and social issues of the sixties, I was fascinated by this dynamic exchange of opinions and longed for the courage to participate. Yet no matter how hard I tried, I still could not speak up. On my first term paper, the professor wrote, "You write and think very well. I'd really like to hear from you in class. I hope you find your voice."

This professor was someone I admired and respected. That he took the time to acknowledge my ability meant the world to me. I made an appointment and asked him to help me understand why it was so difficult to express myself and speak up in class. I don't think he ever understood how much his support helped to change my life.

Determined, inspired, and still scared to death, I went back to class with a plan—just keep trying until the first sound came out. Looking back, I see a frightened young girl hiding her shaking hands under a table. She is taking deeps breaths to calm her fear, praying, shaking, and practicing day after day. Her trembling voice is barely audible, cracking so quietly that for many months, no one takes any notice.

One day I heard a tiny voice. It got louder and louder until others heard it too. The moment I heard the sound of my own voice, I realized that the impossible was possible! Each successful attempt at speaking up gave me more courage to communicate with less effort until finally I could articulate my thoughts with confidence and ease.

Years later I learned that my inability to speak in class was a lesson to prepare me for a greater purpose. A social worker, I saw an enormous need to help women and children who were innocent victims of domestic violence and abuse. Connecting with their loneliness and vulnerability, I became determined to find a way to speak up for people who were too frightened to speak up for themselves.

Every word flows from my heart when I speak on their behalf—and then when I'm complimented on how well I talk in public, I just smile and let my inner light shine.

~ Vivian Clecak

Vivian Clecak, *a respected expert on domestic violence, is executive director and co-founder of Human Options, a multi-service agency for abused women and children in Orange County. She has received many honors including the California Association of Nonprofits Lifetime Achievement Award and the International Conference on Violence and Trauma Lifetime Achievement Award. In addition to her role at Human Options, Vivian also has a coaching practice specializing in work with women leaders.*

www.humanoptions.org

Natalie Cole

Following My Gut

Women have recognized that while we may not have total control over our destinies, we do have a lot of control over our quality of life and to some extent our longevity. The best way to improve quality and quantity is by being well-educated and proactive. Read, listen, use common sense, and follow your gut.

~ Dr. Nancy Snyderman

Ever since junior high school I wanted to be a business owner, but I didn't have any idea what that business could be. I just knew that one day *something* would happen to inspire me to fulfill my dream of becoming an entrepreneur.

When I approached my fortieth birthday, I made a personal goal to be fit and trim by this milestone occasion. My body grew strong and firm, but I could not lose any weight. I became a vegetarian, exercised religiously, and even decided to train for a marathon. Still, the number on the scale refused to budge.

Sharing my frustration with my husband, he suggested that my metabolism was probably slowing down so I tried a variety of ways to ramp it up. When that didn't work, I went to a doctor who said to eat less and exercise more. I went home determined to try harder, but several weeks later I hadn't lost a single pound.

Thinking that I might have a thyroid problem, I went back to the doctor for a blood test. Once again he declared that I was perfectly fine. But then I heard a little voice inside me say, "Something is wrong. It's time to take control and manage your own health." Following my gut, I made an appointment for an ultrasound. Looking back, if I hadn't listened to that little voice, I'm not sure that I'd be here to share my story with you.

The most defining moment of my life was being diagnosed with thyroid cancer. An ultrasound revealed three lumps in my throat— two were benign and one was malignant. I couldn't believe that it had taken two years and a concerted effort on my part to finally get the correct diagnosis and hear someone say, "This is serious."

After an operation to remove my cancerous gland, I had an awakening that inspired me to look at life in a different way. It became clear that I needed to quit my job and launch my dream of owning a business. A senior manager with a successful twenty-four year career in journalism at a large newspaper, I asked myself: "Are you happy, satisfied, and fulfilled? Are you passionate about what you do every day? Are you living the life of your dreams?" The answer to each question was a resounding "no". So I started my own newspaper.

Treat your body with love and respect like you would treat a good friend. Pay attention to the messages that it sends and take immediate action if you hear a little voice say that something isn't right. Ask questions, educate yourself, and become an active participant in all your health care decisions in order to make the choices that are right for you.

My wish is that you will enjoy a long, happy and very healthy life. Please don't wait for a medical emergency to begin living the life of your dreams!

~ Natalie Cole

Natalie Cole *is the founder, publisher and CEO of OurWeekly LA and OurWeekly Antelope Valley newspapers that address topics and issues facing the African American Community; Healthier You, a bi-monthly health magazine, and the founder of the West Coast Expo, a Business, Technology, Sustainability/Green and Health Exposition. She founded the Urban Media Foundation, an after-school journalism & media technology training program for youth.*

www.ourweekly.com *www.urbanmediafoundation.org*

Nina Craft

Becoming a Better Daughter

Most of the other beautiful things in life come by two's and three's, by dozens and hundreds. Plenty of roses, stars, sunsets, rainbows ... but only one mother in the whole world.

~ Kate Douglas Wiggin, children's book author,
started first free kindergarten

One day my mom and I were at lunch overlooking the beautiful Palos Verdes Peninsula, and she casually said, "I am truly happy." I was stunned! This statement was a long time in coming. Hearing my mom say she was happy meant everything to me!

Sometimes, attaining the simple things in life, like happiness, can be a challenge. But the obstacles on the path to happiness weren't my fault. Nor were they my mother's fault. No one was to blame. We were just two people, two adults, learning to relate to one another on a mother-daughter journey that never really ends.

Why did I think that it should have been an easier road to traverse? Perhaps it was my entitlement attitude. I know my parents sacrificed a lot for me to be who I am. But don't most parents? They don't really think we owe them something, do they? How would we pay them back anyway, if we did?

How am I supposed to let my mother know that I love her for risking her life to have me, or for losing sleep because I was ill as a child, or for giving up things she may have wanted to do in order to have time for my chosen activities? I really didn't think that was my problem to solve. I just figured that was what people sign up for when they decide to become parents. And I have to admit that I thought that way for a very long time.

Until one day when I was in my early thirties, my mom looked at me and sighed. I remember thinking, "Great, what did I do this time that didn't meet her high standards?" But all I said was "What?" in anticipation of one more lecture about how I wasn't measuring up. I'm sure that impatience and irritation were evident in my voice, but my mom didn't get defensive at all.

Instead, she made a profound statement. It was profound because not only did it stick with me—it actually shaped the rest of my life. My mom wistfully said, "We put so much time into you girls, and I don't really know how you turned out. I don't hear your conversations. I really don't know how you think."

She wasn't looking to criticize me! That was all in my mind! I suddenly realized that my mom wasn't trying to make me perform to her high standards. She was simply asking to be at the dress rehearsals of my own performances—to be a fly on the wall as I prepped to share my best with others.

I started to think, "Maybe I can ask my mom to hang out with me and my friends when I have planning meetings. I can invite her to meet my friends' moms and we can all go to tea. We can laugh and share trans-generational tips, observations of the past, concerns for the present and hopes for the future. We could take classes together and create together." I could really do this! Suddenly, I felt extremely empowered.

I flashed onto the great bonding that was possible if I listened to this opportunity and cultivated her request into a wish fulfilled. I hugged her and asked if she wanted to have fly-on-the-wall privileges. "Would you enjoy hanging out with me as my friend?" She jumped at the opportunity with an even bigger sigh, but this time it was a sigh of relief. That was the moment when my relationship with my mom totally changed.

Now I warmly call my mom by her first name, interspersed with times of calling her "Mommy." I invite her to lectures followed by dinner to discuss what we have learned. When we have disagreements, I allow myself to see the growth that will develop on the other side of the argument and embrace the full intimacy of allowing each of us to "go there" in our verbal demands and retorts.

My goal has evolved from making a commitment to joyfully fitting my mom into my life, to being available on her time and letting her choose a good day to hang out. The biggest thing I've learned from this is that when someone signs up to be a better daughter, they also sign up to make the sacrifices that lead to a more meaningful and loving relationship.

I'm glad that my mother has become so much more than just a fly-on-the-wall. I look forward to sharing my thoughts with her, even if they are not what she may have anticipated. It is a fun and enlightening adventure. I am overjoyed that we have redefined our mother-daughter relationship and I'm grateful to have the opportunity to spend more time with her.

And because of that, like my mom, I can honestly say that today, I am truly happy too.

~ Nina Craft

Dr. Nina Craft, *Ph.D., M.B.A., aka Dr. Neen, the Think It, Do It! Queen, is an award winning social entrepreneur, international speaker, author, trainer and mentor, as well as radio and television guest. She is the CEO of VisionFocus, a business training and life-balance education company.*

www.ThinkItDoIt.com

Susan Crank

Remembering the Love

If I curl up in a ball and become useless, what am I saying about my son's life? He would want me to live fully ... I'm one of the only things he has left behind, and so if I live... generously and honorably, then I do it as a tribute to him.

~ Elizabeth Edwards

I went into shock when I got the call that said my eleven-month-old son had fallen and hit his head on the floor. The baby sitter had already taken him to the hospital where he was diagnosed with a cerebral hemorrhage. Oh my God! My baby's brain was bleeding!

After two-and-a-half hours of surgery, my husband and I were given the heart-wrenching news. The doctors had done everything possible to save our child, but he didn't survive the operation. Devastated, we went home to grieve the loss of our precious little boy.

I'll never forget the feeling of pure love when baby Todd was placed in my arms for the very first time. He was so beautiful! He took my breath away! Chubby and cuddly, the sparkle in his eyes is what I cherished most.

After our baby died, my world fell apart. I had so many hopes and dreams for Todd! Throughout it all, my husband was my rock. Over and over he said that our son's death was a terrible accident. No one was to blame. Nothing good could come from letting the rest of our lives be destroyed by the tragic loss of our beloved child.

One day after drying my tears, my husband looked into my eyes and tenderly asked, "Do you think Todd would want his parents to crumble with sorrow? Or would he want us to remember all the love?"

"Of course, he would want us to remember the love!" I said. "Remembering the love is absolutely what our little boy would have wanted us to do." This sudden realization put me on a new life path, and in that moment it became clear that I would always be Todd's mom. I needed to make his spirit proud of me.

I continue to honor our son's memory in many different ways— loving his dad, creating a family-like environment at work, nurturing my employees, mentoring young people and always striving to make a difference. Thirty years later, I am still a mother determined to make something beautiful come from the sparkle in my baby's eyes.

~ Susan Crank

Susan Crank is chairman and CEO of the Lunada Bay Corporation that designs and manufactures women's swimwear and active body wear for high-end department and specialty stores. She has received numerous awards including Woman Making a Difference, the Surf Industry's Environmentalist of the Year Award, and the Otis College of Art & Design's Creative Vision Award.

www.lunadabayswim.com

Anita M. D'Aguilar

My Father's Words

It is only when we truly know and understand that we have a limited time on earth and that we have no way of knowing when our time is up, that we will begin to live each day to the fullest as if it were the only one we had.

~ Elizabeth Kubler-Ross

When I was in my mid-twenties, my mother and father died within eighteen months of each other. Each loss knocked me off my core and created an unfathomable void in my world. Both my parents' deaths were followed by periods of deep introspective assessment as I struggled to come to terms with their passing. But the death of Dad, my best friend, my confidant and life-line, completely changed my perspective about living and dying.

My father assumed the role of a single parent for his two little daughters shortly after my eighth birthday. When my mom was unexpectedly taken ill and hospitalized, Dad immediately rearranged his entire life to rear my younger sister and me. Although my beloved father was a man of humble beginnings, he will always be a giant in my eyes.

Colorful and witty, Dad had a sharp mathematical mind and loved quizzing me on multiplication tables and challenging me with math equations just for the fun of it. A graceful man with natural style and class (who sometimes made wardrobe changes a few times a day!) he was an entertainer-of-sorts and always the life of a party. A crowd of people would gather around to watch my father glide his tap shoes across the dance floor with precision and elegance.

Now this man of incredible integrity and honor was gone! My best friend and hero had died — and I was devastated beyond words. Life as I knew it would never be the same.

Preparing for Dad's funeral was the hardest thing I've ever had to do. When I sat down to write his eulogy, my pen would not move. I didn't know where to begin. How could I possibly encapsulate such a precious life on a piece of plain white bond paper and read it aloud in the few minutes allotted in the program? Feeling "stuck" in a very dark place of not wanting to let my father go and not understanding why he had gone, I suddenly thought of my cousin, Marie, and decided to give her call.

Marie had a very close relationship with my father, and I knew she would understand that Dad had cherished his mom the same way that I had always cherished him. I asked my cousin how my father had once found the strength to deal with the grief of his mother's loss. Marie explained that after Dad's mom died, he said: "People Grow Old, People Get Tired — and They Move On."

I was taken aback by the realization that my father had treasured life enough to respect death and dying as a natural part of it. This explained so much about Dad's free spirit and his ability to appreciate every day like it was the last. My father's words resonated within my soul and filled me with strength, encouragement and inspiration. His remark, spoken after the loss of his mother so long ago, gave me peace and became my release. I suddenly realized that my father's spirit wasn't gone. It had simply moved on.

Shortly before Dad died, I accepted a job at a top Stock Brokerage Firm on Wall Street; after his death I was torn about starting the training program so soon. Now, reflecting upon what my father had said to Marie, I decided to honor him by channeling my energy and fervor into creating an exciting new opportunity for myself—exactly as he would have wanted me to do. That was the moment when I instinctively knew everything would be okay. It was time to create my own destiny and start the training program as planned.

"I will give you treasures out of the darkness and riches that have been hidden away …", the Bible tells us. (Isaiah 45:3) Once I made the decision to enter the training program, I never looked back. I became one of the first few female trainees in the Financial Services Industry, a male-dominated business at the time, to make cold calls and land multi-million dollar accounts.

My father's words still cradle my soul, a gentle reminder that I am just passing through this planet called Earth. Too often we don't take the time to appreciate how wonderful the journey can be. That is why I believe it's so important to search your heart for the dream you want to unleash. When you discover what your dream is, give it your all. No matter what happens, never give up!

~ Anita M. D'Aguilar

Anita D'Aguilar *is a Vice President — Investments with UBS, a global financial services company in Los Angeles. Anita has an MBA in Finance and has been featured in financial publications: One Up on Wall Street, Ticker Magazine, and Black Enterprise. Her many philanthropic interests include Honorary Committee for Artists for a New South Africa (ANSA), Friend for Boardroom Bound as well as a host of other civic and church affiliations.*

Martha Daniel

Journey to Freedom

The cause for freedom is not the cause of a race or a sect, a party or a class — it is the cause of human kind, the very birthright for humanity

~ Anna Julia Cooper, African American scholar

I once had a terrifying experience that totally transformed my life. It was the moment when I first grew into the woman I was meant to be.

In 1968, against my mother's wishes, I participated in a march for civil rights in the inner city of Memphis, Tennessee. An African-American junior in high school, I was very curious about what was happening in society and wanted to be part of what was going on. But I was unprepared and horrified by the violence that broke out.

It is still so clear and vivid in my mind — the tear gas, gun shots, looting and shouting. I just kept running and running not knowing where to go or what to do. A teenage boy was shot right in front of me and bled to death in the street. All I could think was, "Why is this happening?" That question took me to another level. "What does freedom really mean?" Something said, "Get a good education and make a plan to leave Tennessee."

I walked fifteen miles from the inner city to my home in a suburban part of Memphis, a safe neighborhood for middle-class African American families. Exhausted and shaken, I reflected on what I had experienced and what I wanted to do with my life. When I opened the door, my mother hugged me in tears asking where I had been and if I was okay.

"Mom," I told her. "I just want to be free." A sharecropper's daughter who had known a much harder life, she said, "But you are free!" Sadly, I explained that I was not. "I don't want to live like this anymore. I want my life to be different — to be educated and successful! Mom, I have dreams! One day I want to be the president of a big company!"

After high school I decided to join the navy because the military was a way for me to leave Memphis and head for the West Coast where I could make my dreams come true. After serving for a year and a half, I received a medical discharge and went to college graduating with honors. Later, I received a Masters Degree in Business Administration.

But the most important lesson is this: on my journey to freedom, I never let thoughts of past discrimination stay in my mind. Learning to understand and appreciate different nationalities and cultures was another way that I educated myself. Today, this is essential to achieving success in America, no matter who you are, or what you do.

~ Martha Daniel

Martha Daniel is the founder, President and CEO of Information Management Resources, Inc, (IMRI), a leading technology and engineering services company in Aliso Viejo. An ordained minister in the African Methodist Episcopal Church, she has received numerous awards for her business acumen and leadership in Los Angeles and Orange County including the National Association of Women's Business Owners Hall of Fame.

www.imri.com

Nancy Davison

The Gift of Dignity

What's right with American women is that they're rearing and provid-
ing for the next generation of Americans while at the same time caring
and providing for the last generation of Americans … I'm convinced
that this Woman's Nation will be able to say that, believe it or not, there
was once a time when there was no cure for Alzheimer's.

~ Maria Shriver, *The Shriver Report*

Women are born leaders. It just comes naturally to us. That is why
what we do is much more important than what we say, especially
when it comes to loving our families and raising our children.

My father-in-law was a victim of dementia or early Alzheimer
disease and found himself in a nursing home where he was very
unhappy and did not want to be. When my husband and I agreed to
bring him into our home one summer, it was a given that most of the
responsibility for his visit would fall upon my shoulders. A working
mom with two active sons under the age of ten, I knew the extra

time required for his care would make life challenging, but I didn't expect it to be so life-changing.

Time with their Grandpa was a blessing to our boys. He participated in all aspects of our family's life, rising every morning at 7:00 am sharp, making his own bed, dressing himself to the tee, right down to the handkerchief in his pocket, and putting on his gentleman's hat for his daily two mile walk. He loved being part of the family.

I even took him and my sons on business appointments with me, all three in dress shirts with a stack of cards. I explained to the receptionist that they needed a place to play while I brokered real-estate deals with CEO's.

Grandpa's favorite hobbies were gardening and oil painting. Taking him to the art supply store one day was a challenging experience for both of us. As I drove, he kept repeating over and over that he couldn't paint any longer. He had been told that he wouldn't remember how. My insistence that he teach me to paint was the way I got him to rethink his ability. It was wonderful watching his eyes light up as he walked around the store carefully selecting everything he would need.

When we arrived home, my father-in-law and I went outside to the patio, and I asked what he was going to teach me to paint. Pensively holding his new paintbrush over a blank canvas, he replied, "Why, the flowers of course! They are very lovely, fragrant and elegant in their simplicity this time of year!" Soon the brush strokes began to flow. That moment will live in my heart forever. He was so happy just to be alive!

Our hearts were broken when Grandpa died later that fall. Wiping away tears, I reflected upon all the different paths my family could have chosen, and I was glad that taking care of him was the choice we made.

My father-in-law's funeral reminded me how precious life is, and it taught my children that giving time to dignify another person's existence is the most elegant gift of all.

~ Nancy Davison

Nancy Davison has been an entrepreneur for over thirty-five years in the real estate field throughout Southern California. Her expansive career has led her to helping seniors with their homes. She is a Real Estate Specialist, REALTOR, along with other designations at Coldwell Banker in Dana Point specializing in South Orange County. Nancy is actively involved in volunteer work serving on non-profit boards and community and school programs.

Donna Deutchman

Finding My Tempo

In the long run, we shape our lives and we shape ourselves. The process never ends until we die. And the choices we make are ultimately our own.

~ Eleanor Roosevelt

Sometimes the wisdom of knowing the difference between reaching an early finish line and walking away can be difficult to explain to the outside world, but to the individual, it is profound. The decision to make a change can be very bold and courageous.

My first early finish line was the result of self-realization beginning in graduate school when I identified the difference between what I thought I wanted to do with my life and who I wanted to be. For most of high school and college, I strategically took classes and jobs related to my goal of earning a Ph.D. in clinical psychology.

I was successful in graduate school, earning straight A's, but realized that I didn't feel genuine in the role of a clinical therapist.

Fully immersed in the university environment for several years, I discovered that devoting my time to research and publishing versus working with clients and people did not fit with my nature and who I really was.

The idea of leaving a Ph.D. program was unthinkable to other students, friends and faculty. I was told that it could bring down the standing of the entire program. To avoid that, I was granted a six-month leave of absence with an option to return.

I realized two things: First, I had actually reached one goal set in my early educational years—completing a degree and several internships. These were complete activities, not only steps toward an end. Second, I needed to "re-purpose" the tools that I had learned and become the best person I could be.

The university offered me a job in the Gerontology Program working on the most cutting-edge programs on healthy aging in the country under the direction of the best leaders and visionaries in the field. This was where I found my tempo! But after nine years of rapid growth and success, the board of directors suddenly shut the door on expansion and initiated a slow-growth policy for new programs. My once dynamic working environment became mired in bureaucratic red tape.

It was abundantly clear that the changing culture of the organization left me with little opportunity in the way of personal mission or professional growth. But this was where I had found my tempo! I had learned that program development and creating new services are instinctive to the very core of my being!

The moment came when I had to choose between resisting my natural calling as a change agent and risking proven success for the "unknown." Unlike graduate school, this time the finish line was drawn unexpectedly compelling a move on my part. I realized that I had already reached the finish line but had missed the sign.

Knowing the institution I had helped to create was no longer able to maximize my talents, I packed my bags and walked away. In this case, the "unknown" was the only path that allowed me stay true to myself. In retrospect, my decision to leave was a blessing. I went on to forge a new career in nonprofit leadership that reflects the person I am today.

I'm not a "company gal" who expects a gold watch or standing ovation for my accomplishments. I'm more of a "JoAnne Appleseed" wanting to look back one day and see how many orchards I have planted and how many families can feed themselves from the fruits of my labor. This is what matters to me.

Find your tempo. Don't be afraid to change course or shift the direction of your life especially in the face of proven success. Stay true to the person you are—and to the one you want to be.

~ Donna Deutchman

Donna Deutchman is the Chief Executive Officer for Habitat for Humanity, San Fernando, Santa Clarita Valleys, a nonprofit that lifts families out of the cycle of poverty housing through homeownership, self-sufficiency skill building and education. A leader in the development of direct services, research, and policy, she has dedicated her career to advancing the missions of non-profit organizations through effective innovation and self-sustaining business practices.

www.HumanityCA.org

Sister Terry Dodge

Driven to Action

And let us not forget the power of anger in the work of justice …
Embedded in the angry demands of social change are the seeds of hope
that the world can be a different and better place.

~ Reverend Mona West

My younger brother and I were always close in spite of a nine year age difference. He was in eighth grade when I left home and entered the convent. Years later if I had met a heroin addict like Joel on the street, I would have been very frightened.

Adolescent peer pressure led my brother into making bad choices such as hanging out with the wrong crowd, using drugs, stealing, and breaking into homes. He was sent to prison for drug-related crimes numerous times, only to be released and then be put behind bars again. But I loved Joel, and I could see the goodness in him.

I was the only family member who visited him in every prison in California, until twelve years later, the day came when I knew he was finally ready to make a change. But Joel was filled with despair thinking there wasn't any hope for someone like him. I remember looking at my brother through a glass partition and hearing him say his life was over.

His words were a shock to my system! This was a total contradiction to my beliefs! I believe in redemption! I believe in change! To witness such despair and to be in the midst of so little hope awakened something inside me. I called several places to see what resources might be available for someone like Joel. Everyone I talked to would only look at my brother's history and all the negative things he had done.

My frustration with the system drove me to action. I remember thinking very consciously that I wanted to dedicate my life to giving people like Joel a second chance. Wouldn't it be great if there was a place where someone could go when they got out of jail, a place that could provide support and encouragement regardless of their past? When I told my brother what I was considering, he said it was a dead-end street.

After Joel was released from jail for the last time, I found a small apartment for him and enrolled him in welding school. Finding work was difficult and discouraging, but once he landed a job, his entire perspective changed. He thrived juggling a forty hour work week and going to school at night. Small moments like these can be life-changing!

Eighteen months after finally getting his life back on track, Joel lost his life in a motorcycle accident. Twenty-three years later, his picture still sits on my desk, a tender reminder that my brother is the reason for the work that I do.

I could have gone back to the convent and to my job as a high school teacher, but my unwavering belief in Joel's potential put me in a new direction. "I believe in you," I say to the next lost soul behind a glass partition. "You can change. You can do things differently. Your past does not determine your future."

~ Sister Terry Dodge, SSL

Sister Terry Dodge, SSL, is the Executive Director of Crossroads, Inc., a residential program for women released from California State prisons, the founder of Turning Points Staffing Services for formerly incarcerated and at-risk women, and the Advocacy Project to support women on parole. She is a fellow of the Women's Policy Institute working to change the policy of shackling pregnant inmates. Sister Terry is the recipient of the prestigious Minerva Award given to women serving on the front lines of humanity.

www.crossroadswomen.org

Kathryn Downing

Finding a Way Forward

In all realms of life it takes courage to stretch your limits, express your power and fulfill your potential …it's no different in the financial realm.

~ Suze Orman

My parents' twenty-plus year marriage was a sad example of what can happen to a woman who finds herself trapped in a relationship without love, caring, or respect because she can not support herself or the children.

A successful engineer, my father used his financial means to control his wife who had very little education and no opportunity for financial independence. He gave her an allowance specifying that a certain amount of money was to be used for clothing, food, and other house-hold expenses. Over the years I watched my mother, who loved fine things, squirrel away money from here and there and take it to a local furniture store.

The delivery truck arrived at our house when I was about fourteen years old. It was wonderful to have a new sofa, a real dining room table and beautiful upholstered chairs instead of folding furniture and hand-me-downs. My mother was thrilled! But when my father came home, he was so angry that I made a personal commitment to never be financially dependent on anyone.

My favorite aunt found herself stuck in an unhappy marriage too. Like my mother, she raised five children and had limited education. Her husband, a dreamer, never finished a single thing he started. Finally, after more than twenty years of unhappiness, the two most important women in my life divorced their husbands and found a way forward.

Although my mother never went beyond eighth grade, she eventually managed to own motels and restaurants, while my aunt, at the age of forty-five, went to law school and graduated as the only woman in her class. After passing the bar, she established her own law firm because no other firm would hire a woman.

Their struggles made me realize how important it was to attend college, but it was disappointing to graduate near the top of my class and not get hired. Every man who interviewed me said that I was a bad investment because after being trained, I would get married, have children and quit my job. These remarks were so hurtful that I decided to follow in my aunt's footsteps and go to law school. Fortunately by the time I was admitted to the bar, firms were beginning to hire women, and I found a job.

Then, about eighteen months into my practice, I woke up one morning and did not want to go to work. I had a law degree and a well-paying job, but I hated what I was doing! I didn't want to be a lawyer! On some deeper level, I had known this all along, but in my quest for financial stability and independence, I had never really thought about doing something that would actually make me happy.

From that moment on, I decided to always have two requirements for my life: financial security and the ability to feel fulfilled by the work I do. I quit my job as a lawyer never imagining that one day I would become president and chief executive officer of the second largest daily metropolitan newspaper in the country.

I made a commitment to making sure that women have full opportunities in all aspects of their lives and creating a work environment where every individual could feel respected. I took these beliefs into each of my organizations, hiring, promoting and encouraging every person in the company — women, men, and people of color.

Every girl and woman needs to know that whatever the circumstances of her life, a good education, courage and commitment are essential to finding her way forward.

~ Kathryn Downing

Kathryn Downing serves as the chairwoman of The Women's Foundation of California and Founder of Galileo Coaching. As a coach and strategic planning consultant, she draws on the knowledge and perspectives gained from more than thirty years of experience in the business world, as well as in nonprofits and as an individual who has made significant career and personal transitions. Kathryn was the Publisher, President and CEO of the Los Angeles Times.

www.linkedin.com/in/kathryndowning

Judy Egenolf

Sharing Jonah's Journey

...education is not what the teacher gives; education is a natural process spontaneously carried out by the human individual ... Human teachers can only help the great work being done, as servants help the master.

~ Maria Montessori

When nursing our first baby, I didn't worry about birth control because my physician had assured me it would be difficult to conceive. The news that I was pregnant again came as a big surprise. Another child at that time would take me away from my long-planned path to graduate from college with a degree in art before expanding our family. I struggled to accept the new direction my life was taking.

Our second child entered the world three months prematurely, and by all appearances, Jonah was a very sick little guy. At ten months he was like an inanimate sack of potatoes and could not lift his head at all. It was devastating to hear neurologists say that our son would not progress according to normal expectations.

I made an appointment to visit a Delayed Development Program for disabled children. "Jonah does not belong here," I thought, observing mechanical behavior between teachers and students. "The jury is still out on my son's potential." This experience motivated me to become a credentialed Montessori teacher and open a little school in my home. I wanted Jonah to be in a learning environment with active toddlers rather than lower-functioning children as role models.

The first day of class started in our small duplex apartment with five other adorable eighteen-month old boys as "students." It didn't take long to realize that my "surprise" baby had not taken me away from my dream; instead his birth had led me to my proper path. I had become a teacher, a musician and an artist! I could incorporate every aspect of my being into teaching. This was exactly what I was supposed to be doing.

I expanded the six-student school in our apartment to three classrooms in a large facility. By the time Jonah was five, we knew that we were a very lucky family. The little boy who would likely "not progress according to normal expectations" went on to become a star volleyball and basketball player with an intellect that was off the charts. Today our son is a successful software consultant and the proud father of two.

Sharing Jonah's journey from disability to success has brought me more moments of joy than I could have imagined. The path created by life is often more rewarding than what we can dream for ourselves.

~ Judy Egenolf

Judy Egenolf, *C.E.S., (Certified Exchange Specialist), is the CEO of Amherst Exchange Corporation which she established with her husband. She has served as Qualified Intermediary in thousands of tax deferred exchange transactions nationwide entrusted with proceeds in the hundreds of millions of dollars. Prior to Amherst, Judy owned and operated Sunrise Montessori Pre-School in Santa Barbara and later taught music performance and art history in kindergarten through sixth grades in the public school system.*

www.amherst1031.com

Kathy Eldon

The Laughing One

A child points out to you the direction and then you find your way.

~ Kenyan Proverb

My son, Dan, had a special way of igniting a "spark" in the heart of anyone who met him. But when he was killed at the age of twenty-two trying to tell the world an important story, the "spark" in my life went out.

My spark had first been lit when my husband and I moved from a drab suburb in London to sun-drenched Nairobi, Kenya, with our two young children, Amy and Dan. A young freelance journalist with the local newspaper, my mind was constantly exploding with new ideas about how to tell stories that could make a difference in my adopted country. Dan loved to trail alongside me when I went on assignments and would often shoot photos for my stories.

Naturally, I was proud when Dan, then twenty-one, traveled into Somalia with a friend from Reuters News Agency to shoot photos of a little-known famine that was raging in the country. His photographs of starving men, women and children, brought international attention to the plight of the hungry Somalis and helped trigger an international response, "Operation Restore Hope," which brought aid to the people.

Over the next year, Dan returned to Somalia again and again, documenting a situation which was rapidly spiraling into a violent civil war led by General Aideed, a ruthless warlord. In June of 1993, deeply concerned about my son's safety, I encouraged him to leave, but he explained that his job wasn't done and he had to remain to tell the story.

On July 12, 1993, United Nations forces bombed a house where it was thought that General Aideed was hiding. The warlord wasn't there, but in the brutal mortaring, seventy-four innocent people were killed and scores of others seriously injured. Survivors rushed to the "journalists'" hotel begging the international correspondents to record the carnage. A small group, including my son, agreed to go, but only if they were accompanied by armed guards.

When the convoy arrived on the scene, more than 1000 people had gathered in the compound of the house. As the journalists began to photograph the dead and dying, the crowd, enraged by deaths of their families and friends, began shouting. Rapidly, a mob formed and turned on Dan and his colleagues, beating and stoning four to death.

When I received the devastating news that my son had been killed, I flew to Nairobi to join hundreds of people gathering to celebrate the remarkable life of this young man. The "Celebration of Life" was to be held on the edge of the Great Rift Valley, the land of his Masai "mother," who had dubbed him "Lesharo," which means "the Laughing One," for his contagious sense of humor and constant smile.

Last to arrive was Dan's beloved Land Rover, a temperamental diva he had named "Deziree" after a tempestuous Italian friend. A symbol of Dan's adventurous spirit, Deziree traveled across Africa on magical safaris, including a journey with fourteen friends across four countries, to bring aid to 14,000 people at a Malawi refugee camp. Deziree never was very reliable, and on the way to her owner's memorial service, the ancient vehicle broke down and literally had to be pushed and shoved to her place of honor near the altar.

After the service, a huge bonfire blazed, commemorating the spark that Dan had lit in other people. When most of the people left, I wandered over to stand next to Deziree. Reaching out to touch her, I felt an enormous wave of despair suddenly wash over me. I would never find happiness again without Dan's brilliant light!

Feeling a tug on my shirt, I looked down to see a small Kenyan boy, one of countless children Dan had befriended. "Don't cry, Kathy," the little boy said. "Please don't be sad!" Reaching into his pocket, he pulled out a toy Land Rover. "This is for you," he beamed. "It will remind you of Dan and make you happy." Knowing how precious the toy was to the child, I was about to say no, until I saw a familiar light in his eyes.

I suddenly realized that Dan's "spark" had not been extinguished—it was living on in his special friend! The child's toy Land Rover was a gift of hope, a declaration that my son's death was not the end, but a new beginning. In that moment I had no idea what my life journey without Dan would be, I only knew my son's radiant light would forever accompany me. Thanking the child with a hug, I tucked the toy in my pocket.

After he left, and as dusk was gathering, I placed the little Land Rover on Deziree's hood, and watched a cluster of Masai children gather. Their eyes sparkled as they stared at the toy. One small boy reached out his hand and stopped to look up at me. I nodded, and gently, his fingers encircled the car, as if enclosing a precious gold nugget.

When they scampered off across the plains with their new treasure, the children's pealing laughter reminded me that the spirit of my son, "Lesharo," the Laughing One, was still very much alive.

~ Kathy Eldon

Kathy Eldon has worked as an art teacher, editor, journalist, author and film and television producer in England, Kenya, and the United States. She is the founder of Creative Visions Productions, a film production company, and Creative Visions Foundation, an international not-for-profit organization that supports "creative activists" who use media and the arts to create positive change in the world around them.

www.creativevisions.org   *www.daneldon.org*

Fay Feeney

A Lesson in Leadership

*Honesty is the cornerstone of all success, without which confidence
and the ability to perform shall cease to exist.*

~ Mary Kay Ash

An important turning point early in my career was telling the CEO
of one of our biggest clients the real reason why he was experiencing a high number of work-related injuries.

At the time I was a young consultant hired to help business
leaders improve the safety, health and environmental aspects of
their company. The CEO had been working with my employer for
several months, and no one had ever explained to him why things
were not getting better. My job was to try to turn things around and
save the account.

The only woman in a boardroom filled with men, I knew the
conversation we were about to have would impact the well-being of
over 3,000 people. "So," the CEO wanted to know, "Why are so
many people being injured at my workplace and what do we need

to do to improve the situation?" The room went still, twenty years ago, when I looked him in the eye and spoke the truth: "The reason people are being injured, sir, is because you, as the leader of this company, do not make the safety of your employees a top priority.

"And because you don't make it a priority," I continued, "the people reporting to you do not make it a priority. Therefore, they don't put much energy into preventing injuries in the first place." Taking a breath, I went on to explain that he was not demonstrating his leadership on that issue, and unless he did, things were not going to change.

I'll never know for sure who was more fearful in the silence that followed — the other men in the room or me. They hadn't heard anyone speak to their boss like this before and were concerned that he was not going to accept my remarks in a positive manner.

I could have watered the message down, or I could have let him save face by taking the approach that it was his managers' responsibility to implement better safety procedures. But I knew that when the person in charge doesn't send a clear message that something is important, then the whole organization responds accordingly.

After a moment or two, the CEO composed himself and thanked me for saying that he had not lived up to his responsibility of protecting the safety of his employees. He expressed gratitude for pointing out the challenges that lay ahead and said he looked forward to working with me. When my knees stopped shaking, I called my employer and said that we not only kept the account, but we had moved to a new level of respect.

It is important to be able to communicate effectively, honestly and directly with people, especially those who are in a position of authority. In this instance, it meant having to muster up all my courage to speak truthfully and with conviction about something that I knew was the absolute truth. As a result, the CEO and I were able to build a professional relationship based on mutual respect and trust.

Good leaders are open-minded and willing to listen. They accept responsibility and acknowledge the influence that their position has on the behavior of others — whether it is in business, within their families, their circle of friends, their community or the world.

~ Fay Feeney

Fay Feeney, Founder and CEO of Risk for Good, is a risk professional helping companies interpret information from customers, investors, and competitors. Fay serves as vice-chair of the American Society of Safety Engineers Foundation that provides scholarships to advance the environmental profession. She has been named to the National Association of Corporate Directors "100 Persons To Watch" in recognition of her work promoting the highest standards of corporate governance.

www.riskforgood.com

JJ Flizanes

Playing Peter Pan

I can't tell you the joy I felt flying in that show…I loved it so. The freedom of spirit that was Peter Pan was suddenly there for me.

~ Mary Martin

For as long as I can remember, I have loved to sing and dance. Because I was very active in music programs from grade school through high school and usually had large supporting roles, I expected to get the lead in the Spring musical during my senior year.

After my professor announced that we were going to do Peter Pan, he looked at me and said: "If you want to be Peter Pan, you have to cut your hair." I was horrified! No way! I was not going to cut my beautiful long blond hair!

This was a touchy subject for me. When I was in fourth grade, my mother cut my hair very short so that it would be easier to manage. But I ended up looking like a boy. I even stayed home from school the next day, heartbroken and crying because I was so mortified. For years I was very unhappy until my long hair grew back.

In shock, I looked at my professor and said, "I will not cut my hair. It is one week before prom. Why can't I wear a wig?" Set in his ways, he smugly replied, "Because Peter Pan is going to fly across the stage, and a wig might fall off. Real actresses change their hairstyles for different roles. If you won't cut your hair, you can play Wendy."

That was the moment I decided, beyond a shadow of a doubt, that I was going to play Peter Pan. I would simply make it impossible not to be picked. Confident and determined, I went home and watched the Mary Martin version of Peter Pan over and over until I mastered every lyric to every song.

On audition day, I arrived "in character"—no make-up, a sports bra under a flannel shirt to appear more boyish—and wearing a wig! After singing the first song, I knew I had captured their full attention. When the audition ended, I was given a bundle of sheet music and instructed to learn the rest of the songs for the final call back. "I don't need to learn the songs," I said handing the music sheets back. "I already know them all."

I played Peter Pan, and I wore a wig. Flying through the air was exhilarating! It felt like pure freedom! With my heart pounding and blood pumping, I was thrilled to use the same fly crew from Broadway. I felt like a real professional actress with the same team guiding me—and my wig did not fall off!

Playing that role was the highlight of my senior year because I learned to tap into the power and energy of my mind. I didn't get handed the part although I had expected to. I had to fight for it, but I would not have fought if I didn't believe that I could do it. I made it happen!

We all have power beyond what we use on a daily basis. Believing in yourself has got to be the first power you exercise because how you think and feel about yourself is the blueprint for how others treat you. In order to get anything in life, you have to believe in yourself. If you can't see it, you can't create it.

~ JJ Flizanes

JJ Flizanes is the Amazon.com best selling author of "Fit 2 Love: How to Get Physically, Emotionally, and Spiritually Fit to Attract the Love of Your Life" and "Knack Absolute Abs: Routines for a Fit and Firm Core." Ms. Flizanes is the director of Invisible Fitness and was named best personal trainer in Los Angeles in 2007 by Elite Traveler Magazine. Her mission is to help men and women feel gorgeous and confident, attract more love and live happily ever after.

www.fit2love.info   *www.invisiblefitness.com*

Sylvia Fogelman

Wednesday's Child

Monday's child is fair of face … Tuesday's child is full of grace …
Wednesday's child is full of woe …

~ Mother Goose

It is said that eyes are windows to the soul, but the gaze of the baby in the playpen was blank. He just stared at me without any trace of emotion. I worked with traumatized children of all ages and had never seen one as sad and hopeless. "We can do better!" I thought angrily. "This little boy deserves so much more! Every child does."

At heart I am a social worker, a caretaker, someone who wants to make sure everyone is okay. I have always believed that every person is worthwhile and redeemable. Years ago I became a real estate developer thinking that building low income housing would satisfy my need to help people but soon realized that I wanted to do more.

By happenstance, I interviewed for a position in foster care. Because of the low pay and heavy emotional burden of working with difficult, victimized children, turnover was high. That is why, in spite of my inexperience, I was offered a job.

My responsibilities included visiting children in the homes of foster families and helping them if they were having problems. It didn't take long to become aware of the chaos and inefficiency in the system, and it was troubling to realize that more time was spent meeting regulations than meeting the needs of the children.

I saw toddlers who endured horrendous experiences — a baby in a body cast, little ones burned and beaten, children used or sold for adult gratification. My cries of "how can anyone do this to an innocent child, especially their own," grew non-judgmental. Some individuals are ill-equipped to be parents, and they lose control of their lives. Others are mentally ill or suffer serious addictions to lessen the pain of their abuse.

I learned to accept people as they are — until the moment I saw the woeful look in the eyes of that hopeless baby boy. "Look at him," his foster mother sighed impatiently. She sat him up in the playpen and watched his limp little body plop over like a rag doll. "He's nothing," she said, "just another drug baby." I noted that the child's physical needs were being met. The baby was clean and well-fed. The woman's house was organized and tidy and had a nice back yard for children to play in. Toys were available, but untouched.

Another boy was doing homework at a table nearby, and the woman said, "You just sit there all day until your work is done." "That one," she told me "is so slow. He'll never amount to anything." She didn't seem to care that the boy could hear her every word.

Two other small foster children were sitting quietly in another room. I've never been a "warm and fuzzy" sort of person, but there was no tenderness, affection or encouragement in this woman's house. If the children were spoken to and treated like this in front of me, I didn't want to imagine what went on when I wasn't there.

Instincts I never knew I had kicked in, challenging me to do something that I had been thinking about—open my own foster and adoption agency. For me, this was a very bold move. I could have fallen flat on my face. But I stayed focused and determined until nine months later my new agency placed its first foster child into a wonderful home.

Nothing is impossible if you set your sights high and refuse to give up!

~ Sylvia Fogelman

Sylvia Fogelman *is the founder, president and chief executive officer of the Southern California Foster Family and Adoption Agency, helping children to become successful adults. Sylvia, a NAWBO Woman of the Year, is the recipient of the Small Business Administration's Advocate of the Year Award and Business Development Award. She has received many other honors for her outstanding commitment to abused and neglected children.*

www.scffaa.org

Renee Fraser

Sharing the Glory

I think of my dad every day — every single day... I constantly hear his voice in the back of my head, and I often wonder, in all I'm doing, if he would be proud of me.

~ Michelle Obama

My father's beautiful mahogany desk is my most cherished possession. With a wonderful green leather face carefully embedded into the solid wood, it looks like it belongs to a member of Congress. This desk, where my father worked as an advertising executive many years ago, is now the centerpiece of my office.

I still remember Dad teaching me to ride a bike. In terms of timing, I was behind all the other kids in the neighborhood. Scared of losing my balance and falling, I couldn't quite get the hang of it. But Dad refused to let me give up. "You can do it," he said pushing me forward again and again.

It was an incredible feeling of accomplishment when Dad let go of the bike for good. Pedaling away all on my own was such a glorious feeling! My father was proud of me! He never stopped believing in my ability!

When I decided to start my own advertising agency, Dad didn't really approve. He had always worked for a large corporation and couldn't understand my entrepreneurial instinct. My father also didn't think advertising was any place for a woman saying that I needed to "wear pants" if I wanted to succeed in a male-dominated industry. Eventually, he grew cautiously optimistic, but sadly, he became ill and never knew how successful I would become.

My family was devastated after Dad was diagnosed with lung cancer. It was supposed to be a simple operation to remove a painful growth on the back of his neck. When the doctors said the cancer had metastasized, I had to look the word up in a dictionary to find out exactly what it meant.

It was impossible to help my mother manage Dad's medical care and grow my business at the same time. Coincidentally, a man who didn't know about my father's cancer approached me and said, "Let's combine our business and form a partnership. My business isn't doing well and yours is. How about collaborating?" Under normal circumstances, partnering with someone whose business was failing was something that I would never consider.

Why should I share the glory? Then I realized that kind of thinking at that particular time would be a huge mistake. It was the right moment to share. When I explained my dad's illness and how I would be less involved for the next several months, the man supported the idea of me spending as much time with my family as necessary. In the end, sharing my success made me a better businesswoman and human being.

Sitting at my father's desk, I appreciate how my father inspired and guided me in ways that I never understood when he was alive. His illness taught me that, just like learning to ride a bike, I can't always do everything on my own. Learning to share the glory can increase success by opening doors to new growth and unexpected possibilities.

But the most important piece of advice I offer from my father's desk is this: Love your family. Make them your top priority. No matter happens, always put your family first.

~ Renee Fraser

Renee Fraser, named one of the "Ten Brightest Women in Advertising" and one of the 50 most influential women in Los Angeles, is president and CEO of Fraser Communications. Renee received her Ph.D. in Psychology from the University of Southern California where she is currently an adjunct professor at the Annenberg School of Communications. A successful radio personality, Renee co-hosts a one hour radio show on the CBS news talk station KFWB in Los Angeles, unfinishedBusinesstips.com.

www.frasercommunications.com

Joanne Funari

Stepping Up to the Plate

You don't get to choose how you are going to die. Or when. You can only decide how you are going to live. Now.

~ Joan Baez

When I graduated college at the age of twenty-one, I was an ambitious over-achiever determined to set the world on fire. Nothing was going to stand in my way!

The oldest of five siblings in a close-knit New York family, I decided to start my banking career in Los Angeles. All my ducks were in a row. Everything was lined up just right. Life was working out according to plan—exactly the way I expected it would.

Then, one day my mother called the office crying so hard that she could barely get the words out: Joseph, my nineteen-year-old brother was on his way to a job interview in Arizona where he was attending college. He was riding his motorcycle…He was wearing a helmet …But there was an accident …A driver made an illegal turn... Oh My God... My good-looking, smart, funny younger brother had been killed!

I dropped the telephone and started to hyperventilate. But then, out of nowhere, an indescribable feeling of strength came over me. Retrieving the phone, I composed myself and calmly said, "Mom, I'm coming home. I will be on the next plane." In that moment I knew that I needed to step up to the plate and help my family through this crisis.

On the airplane I thought about all the things that I would have to do: make arrangements to bring my brother's body back to New York, speak with the police and coroner, organize Joseph's funeral and call his friends. Most of all, I needed to be strong so that I could support my parents and younger siblings without falling apart.

When I returned to my job in Los Angeles, I was a different business woman. I was still very focused on my career, but my brother's death gave me a much deeper appreciation for the value of people. I became more sensitive to the needs of my co-workers especially when they had family issues or concerns. As a manager, I realized that even though a structured system might be in place, things don't always work out according to plan.

Stepping up to the plate and supporting my family through the loss of my beloved brother made me see how strong I really am. His memory inspires me to live life to the fullest and to never forget to tell the people in my life how much I love them.

~ Joanne Funari

Joanne Funari is the President of Business First Bank and Executive Vice President/Chief Lending Officer of Heritage Oaks Bank. As a Founding Member of Business First Bank, Joanne has over thirty years of experience in all facets of banking including lending, marketing, sales administration, and management.

Ashley Gardner

Building a Better Life

One of the most important traits a person can have is to find within themselves the ability to be open to new possibilities. Most people greatly limit themselves and don't see the possibilities in front of them..

~ Joan Lunden

I was born in England when the economy was struggling to recover from the aftermath of World War II. Things were so bad that my father had to work for a week to buy me a new pair of shoes. Dad's reality was food rationing, low wages and a constant struggle to support his wife and three small daughters. Wanting to build a better way of life, my parents decided to move to Toronto, Canada when I was four years old.

Even though we spoke the same language, in Toronto I was conscious that my family was "different." Skinny and shy, I wanted to be like the cute, rich and popular girls. Fortunately, my parents created an environment that made living in Canada seem like an adventure, and I always knew that because we were together, everything would be okay.

After graduating high school, I went back to England to meet relatives I never had the opportunity to know, an experience that proved to be a major turning point in my life. For the first time, I understood the enormous sacrifice my parents had made when they immigrated to a new country leaving everything they knew and everyone they loved.

Their courage made me realize there were no limitations on what I could accomplish with my life. That eye-opening moment taught me that I was in charge of creating my own reality. In order to be successful, I needed to believe in myself and be willing to take risks too. When I went back to Canada, I thanked my parents for the huge gift their courage had given me.

Two years later, I fell madly in love and followed the man of my dreams to Vancouver, but after I became pregnant, he fell out of love with me. When he took off for India, I thought, "This is the reality I have created, and I need to accept responsibility for the choices I've made. What can I do with $40.00 to build a better life for my baby and me?"

I bought a one-way ticket to California for $38.50. Some people I knew gave me a place to stay, and I cleaned their house to pay rent. Later, I got a job in a hospital cafeteria making sandwiches until I was promoted to cashier. It wasn't easy being a young unwed mother in America in 1968, but I knew that if I failed, I would pick myself up and try again.

After giving birth to a daughter, I wondered, "What is my job as a mother of this new little person?" The answer that came to me was: "My job is to raise an independent, self-sufficient, young woman who can figure things out for herself and do everything she wants to do to the point where, if I'm not able to be around, she will be okay." Self-confidence was the most selfless gift that I could give to the new little person that I brought into the world.

I have proudly succeeded in my quest. Today, my grown daughter possesses a special kind of inner strength and is a smart, savvy, confident business leader, wife and mother.

When women say to me, "I can't do that," my response always is, "How do you know? You can't be sure until you try!" I tell them my story about the time I heard a voice on the radio say, "You too can become an announcer!" Without any hesitation or experience, I suddenly knew that I could become a radio announcer. Guess what? I did!

Be willing to follow your dream and take a risk. Don't let fear hold you back. There is something to be said about having the courage to walk through a door that opens, a door that maybe you never even knew was there.

The adventure of life is filled with unlimited possibility. You just need to believe in yourself enough to know that that whatever risk you chose to take, one way or the other, you're going to come out of it a better, smarter and happier person.

~ Ashley Gardner

Ashley Gardner is the Executive Director of the Women's Museum of California in San Diego, served on the Commission for the Status of Women for 10 years, and was active in creating the San Diego County Women's Hall of Fame. She is a former actress, local television host and producer, radio announcer, and the founder of Earth Visions Productions, a nonprofit video production company.

www.whmec.org

Tamara Garfio

Giving My All

Teachers, I believe, are the most responsible and important members of society because their professional efforts affect the fate of the earth.

~ Helen Caldicott, Australian physician & author

Deep in my heart is the joyful feeling of knowing that I was born to be a teacher. No matter what may be going on in my personal life, whenever I enter a classroom and shut the door, it's just me and my students on a journey together to conquer the world.

Never a day goes by when I'm not filled with awe seeing the potential of my precious little learners. In many ways I see my job as their teacher the same way that I view my role as a mother of three — to nurture, to guide and believe in them — and to respect each child for their unique abilities.

As a brand-new teacher eleven years ago, one of my fourth graders was an extremely shy little girl who would not participate in class despite my best attempts to engage her. She appeared to be a struggling student, slightly below grade level, and not very interested in learning. During my first parent-teacher conference, it was difficult finding the right words to describe the child's lack of motivation to her mother.

As I was reviewing the little girl's report card, her mother took my hand and stopped me. Leaning closer she said, "Thank you so much. I know you see my daughter struggling, but I want you to understand that she is very motivated and loves coming to school. She returns home excited to read and eager to do her homework. Your positive, happy attitude in the classroom is making all the difference in my daughter's life."

I didn't want this woman to see me cry, nevertheless, my eyes welled with tears. The student's mother went on to explain that she had seen a complete change in her little girl. I will never forget her words: "There are many emotional issues going on at home, but because of you, my daughter is so much more alive. Every day I watch her blossom."

That moment made me realize that success is never contingent upon instant gratification. It means patience, persistence, plugging away and giving my all to the work that I was born to do. As I tell my students, "Life is an exciting journey! We are on the right road! Are you ready? Let's go!"

~ Tamara Garfio

Tamara Garfio is a fourth grade teacher at Maywood Elementary School, one of the few public K-5 elementary schools in California to receive a distinguished GreatSchool Rating of 8 out of 10. Tamara, a graduate of California State University Fullerton, is the 2010 recipient of the prestigious Milken Educator Award given to outstanding educators across the country.

Darlene Gartrell

Words of Wisdom

With every experience, you alone are painting your own canvas,
thought by thought, choice by choice.

~ Oprah Winfrey

I remember my first court appearance as a new attorney like the back of my hand. "Good Morning Your Honor. My name is Darlene Gartrell representing the City of Los Angeles." I did an outstanding job considering that I only said a few words and had practiced them a thousand times.

The judge asked me two questions, and I replied, "Yes, Your Honor. No, Your Honor." That was the extent of the appearance. It was terrifying to face the bench not knowing if the course I was recommending for my client was the best way to win the case.

I hadn't really understood the responsibilities of being a new lawyer when I worked as a paralegal for a small litigation firm. After passing the bar, clients were asking me for legal advice. Two months later I thought, "I can't do this! I have made a terrible mistake! I've got to get out!" Feeling overwhelmed and locked into a career that I didn't enjoy, my self-confidence plunged.

One day my mother saw me crying and asked what was wrong. I explained that I didn't have all the answers for my clients and was scared to be entrusted with so much responsibility. "Darlene," she said, "you have invested a lot of money, blood, sweat and tears into passing the bar. You can stay in the legal profession unhappy and fearful, or you can embrace the privilege of being an attorney and do great things.

"And if it doesn't work out, guess what! That's okay! It's a big world! There's a host of other things you can do. If you don't like the direction your life is taking, you can always switch gears and do something else."

She was right! I didn't have to stay in a job where I was unhappy. I decided to take the bull by the horns and never allow myself to feel intimidated or insecure again. It was empowering to realize that I am the artist of my own life. If I didn't succeed in what I was doing, I could try again or do something different.

My mother's words of wisdom set me free. I had allowed myself to become engulfed by fear. And in that moment of clarity I knew that I wanted to stay in the legal profession after all.

~ Darlene Gartrell, Esq.

Darlene Gartrell, a Senior Vice President at Aon, the leading global provider of risk management services, insurance and reinsurance brokerage, and human resource and benefits consulting, is a highly experienced executive liability claims professional. She has been recognized as one of Diversity MBA magazine's 2010 Top 100 Under 50 Diverse Executives & Emerging Leaders..

www.aon.com

Sharon Gelman

What Good People Do

What I want is so simple, I almost can't say it: elementary kindness.
Enough to eat, enough to go around. The possibility that kids might
one day grow up to be neither the destroyers nor the destroyed.

~ Barbara Kingsolver, author

When I was four, my father drove us downtown to witness all the people gathering for the 1963 March on Washington. I'd never seen so many human beings together in one place. Most of them were black but many, like me, were white. I asked something along the lines of, "But if it's a march for black people's rights, why are there white people here?" I remember my mother's words exactly. She said, "That's what good people do, we stand up for each other."

My parents did not want their children to take part in a protest that might escalate into violence so we went back home to Maryland. My mom stayed with my sister and me while my father returned to the city, joining the historic march where Martin Luther King gave his *I Have a Dream* speech.

It's no wonder I became enthralled with the whole peace, love and protest spirit of the 1960s. I was riveted by TV footage of the freedom rides, civil rights marches and student rallies. From the safety of our living room, I watched fierce dogs, fire hoses and tear gas unleashed on peaceful protestors. My parents took us to rallies of the less volatile sort, efforts to free Soviet Jewry or support liberal politicians. Eventually, my older sister was allowed to go with her friends to antiwar marches and I was wildly impatient to do the same.

When I was fourteen, I spent the summer at a progressive Jewish summer camp modeled after a kibbutz. One of the counselors told us that many people who harvested the food we ate were Mexican immigrants working in terrible conditions, exposed to poisonous chemicals. It was disturbing to learn that kids younger than me worked all day in the fields right here in America.

After camp, I signed up for a United Farm Workers' picket of a local chain supermarket. The call was for shoppers to stop buying grapes and iceberg lettuce until the growers guaranteed better conditions for the farmworkers. That day, I dressed with extra care because I wanted adult shoppers to take me seriously. It was warm out, so I selected a lightweight outfit that looked good against my skin, which was deeply tanned from a summer spent outdoors. My dark hair fell in loose waves down my back. I felt radiant with purpose.

My friend and I positioned ourselves on either side of the store's entrance, holding up signs with the UFW eagle that said "Boycott Grapes." As housewives walked in and out of the glass doors, we asked them to please support the farmworkers. Most of the women ignored us; a few asked questions. Only a few promised to honor the boycott. Clearly, this changing the world business was going to be more challenging than I'd imagined.

After about an hour, one woman who exited the doors looked straight at me and scowled. She stomped away yelling over her shoulder, "Go back home to Mexico where you belong!" Her hatred seared though me. I was stunned into silence. I thought: *You don't hate me. I'm a white kid from Potomac. I live in this neighborhood, just like you.*

I wondered how her words would have felt if my family had come here from Mexico instead of Eastern Europe. Images flashed through my mind: Brown girls picking fruit in the hot sun as they breathed in toxic insecticides; police dogs biting black teenagers dressed in their Sunday best; elderly Jews rounded up and shoved into cattle cars. I was pierced by how irrational and commonplace and terrible prejudice was. At that moment, my mother's words came back to me, like they have many times since: "That's what good people do, we stand up for each other."

Much of my life has been spent working alongside and on behalf of people denied their basic human rights. I've had the privilege of working with remarkable grassroots leaders and movements in oppressed communities and of witnessing the great power that is unleashed when we stand up together for equality and justice.

~ Sharon Gelman

Sharon Gelman is a writer and the executive director of Artists for a New South Africa. Founded to support South Africa's quest for freedom, ANSA now works to combat HIV/AIDS, advance human rights, and preserve the legacies of those who freed their nation from apartheid. Sharon is the producer of the award-winning audiobook Nelson Mandela's "Favorite African Folktales." Recent publications include an essay in "Tutu: Authorized" and the afterword for the unabridged audiobook of Mr. Mandela's autobiography, "Long Walk to Freedom."

www.ansafrica.org

Marilyn Gevirtz

The Sun Still Shines

One day at a time is enough … don't look back and grieve the past, it's gone, don't be worried about the future, it has not come yet… live in the present and make it so beautiful it will be worth remembering.

~ Author Unknown

I often think about a quote from *Frida*, a movie based upon the life of Mexican artist, Frida Kahlo who, at the age of eighteen, suffered a serious injury in a bus accident. Unable to afford medical care, she became increasingly disabled as the years went on.

At the end of the film, Frida is asked how she has been able to endure such intense physical suffering in addition to the emotional pain of her husband's many infidelities. Her answer was: *At the end of the day, we can endure much more than we think we can.*

These simple words stunned me with the powerful truth. I was enduring the two worst things that had ever happened in my life: the death of my younger daughter in 1999 and the death of my husband in 2001. I had always believed the overwhelming grief would kill me, but in that moment I realized—it had not. I found comfort knowing that I had actually endured, however reluctantly, far more than I ever thought I could.

Was my "reluctant endurance" worth it? In the beginning, there were days when I didn't think it was. For the most part, now I can say that life, even without the husband I adored and the daughter I cherished is a gift.

I experience happiness in the loving and the being loved by all those so dear to me, by being able to help people who need it, and by appreciating the joy of a beautiful day. While the sun in my heart may not shine as brightly as it once did, it still shines, and for that I am very grateful.

~ Marilyn Gevirtz

Marilyn Gevirtz *and her late husband shared an intense belief that only an educated population could produce the kind of country we all believe in. After returning from Fiji where Don had served as ambassador in the mid 1990's, they endowed the University of California Santa Barbara Graduate School of Education, now known as the Gevirtz Graduate School of Education, where Marilyn remains active on the Dean's Council. Her other passion is trying to improve animal welfare, a passion that goes back to her earliest childhood memories.*

Patti Giggans

A Woman's Right

My practice has become my reflection, a mirror for me to see my life.

~ Valerie Lee

My martial arts training began in Vietnam where my then journalist husband was on assignment during the war. When we relocated to Paris, I studied karate under a Japanese master who taught in French. The only American, and the only female, in a class of unwelcoming French men, I often went home in tears.

My husband would look at me and say, "This is torture. Why don't you quit?" I tried to explain that I cried out of frustration. The men didn't want to practice with me—they only wanted to prove they could overpower me. But I instinctively knew this was something that I needed to do, so I went back. Little by little, some of the men took me under their wing, and we became allies. I was proud to be the first woman to get a black belt under my Japanese master!

I had yet to discover that martial arts is more profound than learning skills to defend yourself in the terrifying instant when you might need to take action and save your life. Then one day, crossing a street in the middle of Paris, I found myself suddenly surrounded by four men who wanted me to get into their car. One man held a knife. Putting it to my throat, he said, "Come with us."

Instead of panicking, I became calm and centered and said, "Put that knife away. I am not afraid. I am not going anywhere with you. Leave me alone and go away right now." Every time they ordered me into the car, I repeated these same words. Finally, one of them said to the others, "This chick is not afraid of us, let's go." "That's right," I thought with my heart pounding in my chest, "this chick is not afraid of you."

When I told my karate teacher that I needed to give the black belt back because I had only talked my way out, he said, "Are you kidding me? Now you really earned a black belt! You saved your life without having to make a fist!" Ever since then my career has been devoted to empowering women and helping to end violence against them.

Self-defense is more than a woman acquiring skills to protect herself from an attack. It is about self-esteem, autonomy, and being able to use our bodies to manage whatever emotional issues may be going on in our heads. By becoming masters of our own lives, we can take our place in the world as compassionate, engaged leaders in the community.

I still use my years of martial arts training as a doorway into personal self-reflection. Now I practice Zen meditation which enables me to try to be fully present in every moment of my life and to not become constricted by the actions and opinions of others.

It is a woman's right to feel safe, self-confident and empowered. I believe it is also her personal responsibility.

~ Patti Giggans

Patti Giggans, a national expert on sexual and domestic violence, is the Executive Director of Peace over Violence, a multicultural nonprofit organization that focuses on crisis intervention, healing from violence and social change through community activism. Patti has received numerous honors and awards for her outstanding work including the prestigious California Peace Prize and the Lifetime Achievement Award from the California Partnership to End Domestic Violence.

www.peaceoverviolence.org

Debbie Gregory

The Winning Ticket

No matter what you do, make a difference; leave a mark on the places you have been.

~ Wilma Vaught, US Air Force, Brigadier General

Every year I go on a retreat with the courageous widows and families of fallen American soldiers. These women never cease to inspire me, and they always prove to be absolutely amazing in every sense of the word.

Meeting and bonding with military families is the best part of what I do. Their remarkable inner strength and sense of purpose helps to make me a better person. I easily relate to them because I understand that losing someone you love as a result of serving our country is the biggest sacrifice a family can make.

My father, a World War II veteran, will always be my hero. Enduring literally dozens and dozens of operations after returning from battle, he spent too much of his life in hospitals until dying of a service-related disability in a Veterans Hospital over twenty years ago.

Dad always said his glass was half full, not half empty. He never felt sorry for himself and believed he had more than enough to be grateful for. One of eleven children, he had eight brothers serving our country at the same time, and every one came back alive.

As small children, my sister and I would stay with relatives for months at a time so my mother could be with dad every day. When I was old enough to go to the hospital, I was told that if I wanted to visit my father, I wasn't allowed to cry. As a teenager, I became a volunteer for the hospital, and as a young adult, I visited him every single day for years.

Although my father had numerous operations that his doctors thought he might not survive, Dad proved them wrong and pulled through. The toughest part for me was when the doctors eventually had to amputate my father's arm. Again, my dad was my hero. He never indulged in self-pity, saying he didn't have time for it. In spite of his disability, he learned to play the organ beautifully and continued to garden. I didn't know the day would come when the memory of my father's bravery would help me during my own time of need.

That day occurred after a routine mammogram. Waiting for what seemed like an eternity, the doctor entered the room and said. "Well, I have bad news, and I have good news. The bad news is that you have breast cancer. The good news is that we caught it early." But I only heard the word cancer. My immediate reaction was terror and fear.

After seeking multiple opinions, I opted for six months of chemotherapy, three months of radiation, and went shopping for a wig in preparation for the dreaded moment when my hair would fall out. Although I knew it would happen, when it did, I was devastated. Alone in the family room for a private pity party, I tried to distract myself by reading the Sunday morning newspaper.

I decided to check the numbers on a lottery ticket I had purchased on a whim the night before, the first lottery ticket I ever bought. I won $25,000! If I had gotten one more number, it would have been $10 million dollars, but like my dad I thought, "My glass is half full." My winning ticket was more than enough, and I took it as a sign that more good luck was on the way.

Drawing upon the strength of my father, I battled my cancer as if I was fighting a war. I dealt with the fear by taking responsibility for my health and educating myself about the disease in order to make the best decisions and save my life. Cancer took my hair, but not my identity or my sense of purpose.

So here I am, more than ten years later, with my cup overflowing. I am a proud cancer survivor, wife, mother, and CEO of a successful business that supports the amazing men and women of our military, past and present, who make sacrifices for the finest country in the world.

~ Debbie Gregory

Debbie Gregory is President and CEO of MilitaryConnection.com that offers one of the most comprehensive directories of military and veteran resources on the web. MilitaryConnection.com, named one of the elite Top 100 employment websites, works with a multitude of nonprofits, providing resources and facilitating connections with corporations. Debbie is a BRAVO Award Winner presented by the National Association of Women Business Owners in Ventura County.

www.MilitaryConnection.com

Linda Griego

A Quantum Leap Forward

The woman who does not see forward will be left behind.

~ Aurora Sanchez Griego (1909-2003)

My decision to run for mayor of Los Angeles, the second largest city in the country, was a pretty bold move for someone who grew up in Tucumcari, New Mexico where most Hispanics dropped out of school.

While I was growing up, I worked with my family in the local bakery and small grocery store. My grandmother worked in that bakery too—hard physical labor—for forty years. She was my mentor, best friend, and the smartest person I've ever known although she never went to high school. My grandmother instilled in me the belief that no matter what happened, if I followed my heart, I would always succeed.

"La mujer que adelante no mira, atras se queda," my grandmother would say. "The woman who does not see forward will be left behind."

I was the first person in my family to graduate high school. My first grade teacher must have followed my progress because upon graduation her husband, a U.S. Congressman, offered me a job in Washington D.C. Imagine going from high school in a small rural town to working in a Congressional office in the nation's capital! For the next eight years I worked full-time, attended college and graduated with a B.A. from UCLA.

When I accepted a challenge to enter a business-training program offered by an AT&T "baby bell" company to train women for historically male management positions, I learned the nuts and bolts of telephone installation that included climbing telephone poles. My first assignment was chief of an all-male crew. Later, I was promoted to managing a garage of work crews. These empowering experiences gave me the confidence to fulfill a dream—to open my own business.

I left the telephone company to make my dream a reality and started with a small take-out restaurant that was the inspiration for founding my first restaurant. Engine Co. No. 28 is an historical landmark, an abandoned 1912 firehouse, that my partners and I purchased from the city and converted into restaurant and office use. More than twenty years later, my first venture as an entrepreneur is still a popular, well-known restaurant in downtown Los Angeles.

In 1990 I was recruited by Mayor Bradley to be one of two Deputy Mayors. One of my responsibilities was economic development of the city that was in the midst of a deep recession. Thousands of jobs had been lost, and local businesses were struggling to stay open. The horrific 1992 civil unrest following the Rodney King verdict greatly worsened the city's economic downturn. It was devastating to watch my city fall apart.

When the Mayor announced his intention not to run for another term, I was approached to stand for election. I was stunned by this overture! I had never run for public office; the deadline for declaring candidacy was at hand; I had no campaign organization and no campaign funds had been raised. But I felt confident that if elected, my business and government background ideally positioned me to lead Los Angeles forward. Taking a deep breath, I decided to give it my all—and entered the race!

I didn't win the election, but my candidacy was a quantum leap forward for me personally. Never before was every waking moment (and even dreams) filled with such activity! Walking different neighborhoods was an opportunity to get to know my community from the inside out. Each tough debate improved my public speaking skills and increased my visibility in the community. Every day felt like I was running a marathon, but I was continuously invigorated by the support of so many amazing people!

The experience of running for public office and my exposure to business, religious, charitable and other community leaders prepared me for other exciting leadership opportunities that immediately followed. The things that I had wanted to do as mayor, I actually got to do—but in very different ways.

My grandmother was right. If you follow your heart, you will always succeed. Life is a journey, and one experience prepares you for the next.

~ Linda Griego

Linda Griego is President & CEO of Griego Enterprises, Inc., a business management and development company. After serving as Deputy Mayor, she became President and CEO of Rebuild LA, created to jumpstart economic development after the 1992 civil unrest. She also served as President & CEO of the Los Angeles Community Development Bank. Linda has served on many government commissions and boards of directors and currently sits on the board of several nonprofit, profit and private corporations.

Reverend Gwynne M. Guibord

The Voice

For everything there is a season, and a time for everything under heaven.
a time to be born, and a time to die;
a time to plant, and a time to pluck up what has been planted.

~ Ecclesiastes 3

In life, my younger sister, Cindy, was a stunningly beautiful woman. Her beauty was so extraordinary, that whenever she walked into a room, everyone would turn around to look at her. In spite of a twelve year age difference, we were very close, and I adored her.

My sister lived in Michigan, but she would visit me every Thanksgiving, our special time together. There was even a guest room in my house that was affectionately referred to as "Cindy's Room."

When she was diagnosed with myelocytic leukemia at the age of thirty-six, our family was devastated. I was present for every procedure that Cindy had prior to, during and after a painful bone marrow transplant. Despite the transplant, her disease progressed rapidly, and a few months later, my once beautiful sister, was barely recognizable. After she died, my heart was so broken that I didn't think I could take another breath.

The morning she passed away, I left the hospital and went home to call our parents, family and friends. Having been with Cindy around the clock for several days, I was beyond exhausted and needed to lie down. It was then that I felt my sister's presence. Looking up, I saw her spirit walk out of her room and pause at the door of my bedroom. I instinctively knew not to disturb her as she moved on down the stairs.

For several weeks I didn't tell anyone about my experience. At first I told myself that, overcome with exhaustion and grief, I had been hallucinating. My mind had simply created something that I wanted to be true. After wrestling with 'what to do' with what I saw, I ultimately came to the conclusion that what I had witnessed was real.

Three weeks later, at exactly 3:00 am, I was awakened by a Voice that said, "Gwynne, now that this has been revealed to you, I am asking you to be in my service." The same thing happened every morning at the same time for many weeks.

At first I was so terrified that I thought I was having a complete nervous breakdown. Eventually, I started to argue with the Voice saying, "You've got the wrong person. I have a successful practice as a family therapist. My life is going well. Leave me alone. Go away and find somebody else." But the Voice was clear and unrelenting.

One morning, I woke up and a deep feeling of gratitude washed over me as I looked around my beautiful home and back yard. Out loud I said, "All my life I have told You that I love You, and if You are asking me to do this one thing, I'd better show up and do the work." Within a month, I was in seminary.

I was in my late forties when I entered the seminary. It had been many years since I was in school. It was very challenging to read four or five theology books a week and write all the papers required, but at the same time, it was joyful. As a result, I have been ordained an Episcopalian priest and my life has opened in ways that I could never have anticipated.

Prior to that, if someone would have told me that I would end up being a priest who started a nonprofit interfaith organization, traveled all over the world, spoke with Pope John Paul II, and addressed the National Council of Churches twice, I would have responded, "No way! This is not my life." Now I say, "This is my life because God is working through me."

Not a day goes by when I don't miss my sister. But a miracle came out of her death, and for that I am very grateful. What I saw in that moment was real. Cindy was restored to her beautiful self, and her spirit lives.

~Reverend Gwynne M. Guibord

Reverend Dr. Gwynne M. Guibord is the founder of The Guibord Center — Religion Inside Out, an independent California non profit corporation and a place of meeting and interaction for an extraordinary variety of spiritual and religious traditions. Its Mission Statement is to bring people together, to challenge assumptions, unleash the Holy, and affirm the faith that transforms the world.

www.theguibordcenter.org

Jennifer Smith Hale

The Reason Why I'm Here

I knew it was going to be the most extraordinary thing in my life. But how powerful it is, you can never know until you have a baby.

~ Celine Dion

Nothing forces you to reassess your priorities faster than a frightening medical diagnosis. When I was thirty, a rare tumor was discovered on one of my ovaries, large enough and serious enough for doctors to say that I needed to have surgery immediately.

After getting married at the age of twenty-three, I worked in our family's television business but soon discovered that magazines were my passion. The next few years were spent transforming a regional publication into a successful local lifestyle magazine. It was so well-received that I was driven to create a similar one for the entire state.

My mantra regarding motherhood was "in a couple of years, in a couple of years." Obsessed with giving birth to the magazine in my head, every second of my life was devoted to figuring how to turn my concept into reality. At thirty, I still wasn't ready to have a child.

Even after meeting with cancer specialists, my only focus was the magazine in my head. On the day of surgery I suddenly realized what I might have to give up. Just before being taken into the operating room, a nurse approached me and said, "You need to sign here so we can remove your ovaries if necessary." It felt as if I had been struck by a bolt of lightning! I might not be able to have a baby!

It was the most intense experience I've ever had. I could almost hear God say, "You must start to focus on the reason why I brought you here. I have given you the opportunity to be creative and successful, but there is a child waiting to be born to you."

In that moment I knew that I had a daughter out there in the universe! It became clear that after surgery I would need to focus all my attention on bringing her into the world. In the operating room, I begged and pleaded with the doctor to save an ovary, and she said, "I promise to do my best."

My story has a happy ending. The tumor was benign and my ovaries were save. Today I am ecstatic to be the mother of a daughter who fills my life with unimaginable joy. I still work hard and love my career, but my child is my priority and she always comes first.

~ Jennifer Smith Hale

Jennifer Smith Hale is the president, publisher and editorial director of Santa Barbara Magazine and the founder and editorial director of C Magazine, the first luxury lifestyle magazine encompassing the state of California. She is on the board of Smith Media, a company that runs medium market Television stations across the United States. Jennifer was awarded the Dream Foundation's "Outstanding Corporate Sponsor 2006" and was also honored as "Woman of the Year 2010" by Friendly House.

www.magazinec.com

Mary Ann Halpin

The Miracle Baby

Bless you, my darling and remember you are always in the heart — oh tucked so close there is no chance of escape — of your sister.

~ Katherine Mansfield, author

My grand entrance into the world was through a pregnant teenager whisked off to a maternity home run by nuns. Ten days earlier, another mother gave birth to a baby in a hospital a few miles away. But their daughter, Mary Elizabeth, was born with multiple physical disabilities and serious brain damage.

The woman and her husband made the difficult decision to put their newborn daughter into private care. Then, believing it was impossible to conceive again, the heartbroken couple quickly signed up to adopt a child.

The head nun at the maternity home wasn't sure they should be given a healthy baby to replace their damaged one. When the woman got on her knees and promised to love me as if I were her own, the nun said she needed to pray for the wisdom to make the right decision. Two days later, I became my new parents' "Miracle Baby."

I was given lots of love and attention. But was I a "Miracle" or a substitute daughter? Sometimes it felt as if I was living in another little girl's shadow, like an enigmatic twin sister whom my parents never discussed. It wasn't until I was in my mid-forties that I decided to join them on their annual trip to Illinois to visit her in a nursing home. I was somewhat nervous because I was told that it would be very hard to look at Mary Elizabeth, still in diapers, unable to see, sit up, stand, clothe or feed herself.

When I saw her for the first time, I was very surprised. She was absolutely adorable! Mary Elizabeth looked like a sweet twelve year old. Dressed in a little sailor outfit with a bow in her light brown hair, she was sitting in the middle of a small, inflated rubber boat on the floor in her room so that if she rolled over, she wouldn't get hurt.

Everyone adored Mary Elizabeth. One of the youngest patients in this nursing home for the elderly, her body was tiny and her skin was beautiful and soft. The nurses explained that this extraordinary human being was their baby. They glowed when they were around her. It struck me how Mary Elizabeth had affected so many people on such a deeply profound level — and in that moment I realized that *she* was the Miracle Baby.

I spent a lot of time caressing and holding her. When she sat on my lap in her bed playing with a chain bracelet on my wrist, the nurses said they had never seen Mary Elizabeth become comfortable this quickly with someone she had just met.

Later, we sat together near a piano in the recreation room. I put her hand on the keys and she took it away. When I placed her hand back on the piano, she took it away again. Then I put my face near her face and said, "Who is in there? Who are you? Do you know who I am? Mary Elizabeth, if you know who I am, then put your hand on the piano keys now." She lifted her hand and gently placed her fingers on the piano keys.

When I got back to the hotel, I noticed that my bracelet was gone. I can't imagine how she did it. I only understood there was a part of her that needed to have a part of me. On some level, I know in my heart that she and I will always be sisters.

Mary Elizabeth wasn't supposed to live beyond the age of fifteen, but she died at fifty-four. Many people would say that she didn't have much of a life, but I know it was a life of value because she brought so much joy to her world.

In my photography business, I have coined the phrase, "Celebrate your Life as Art." In retrospect, I can trace this phrase back to meeting my sister. She is the reason why I am so passionate about celebrating every day and living every moment to the fullest.

~ Mary Ann Halpin

Mary Ann Halpin is a renowned Los Angeles photographer, speaker and workshop facilitator. She created four photo/essay books: "Pregnant Goddesshood: A Celebration of Life," "Fearless Women: Midlife Portraits," "Fearless Women ~ Fearless Wisdom" and "Fearless Women, Visions of a New World."

www.fearlesswomenglobal.com

Cynthia Harnisch-Breunig

The Canvas of Life

You can't be brave if you've only had wonderful things happen to you.

~ Mary Tyler Moore

With the vision of the lens of time, you are able to see patterns of understanding and have a clear grasp of who you are as a woman, what is important to you, what your values are, and how you can lead a life of value and meaning shaped by insight and wisdom.

I believe that women are the Velcro of the earth. I am mothered, and I mother in return. We are all about relationships; for us, it's all one organic, holistic piece of life. I learned this from my mother who, before she died, was my best friend. A Navy Captain's wife, she was the one who stayed in touch with the families when their husbands and dads were at sea. I grew up hearing my mother say, "Be brave. You can do this. It's okay. Just take it day by day."

One of the paths of my life journey took me into Los Angeles' skid row, heart of the homeless capital of America. Driving through the neighborhood on my way to work, I watched young mothers, children in hand, stepping over trash and walking around people either passed out or sleeping on the street, as they walked to school. As a mother myself, I knew they had the same hopes and aspirations for their children as I had for my son.

At that time I was leading an arts program for children in the inner city. A painter by training, sometimes, I needed to go and paint with the kids just to refocus and remind myself what is really most important. I have come to believe that all children are gifted and talented. Sitting down and painting with them was one of the best things that I could have done for myself.

One day, a shy little girl came over to me as I stood in front of a blank canvas wearing my painter's smock. I was looking around the room, thinking, with my brush poised to begin. She must have noticed my hesitation because she leaned over and whispered in a quiet, mothering way, "Be Brave."

I thought, for me, this is so true! It was such an analogy for my life and what is possible working with these children. Life is a blank canvas and every stroke of the brush is a beginning. Sometimes, we just have to be brave and take a leap forward.

Even at her young age, this little girl knew that it takes courage to create something new. She was already to the point of reaching into her own deeper self willing to take a chance to give birth to that which didn't yet exist. Instead of experiencing the joy of splashing color on the canvas of our lives, we often stop and hesitate.

Painting with this little girl who lived on skid row reminded me that at every moment we must always be our authentic selves. Her mothering words were like an echo from my past. "Be brave. You can do this. It's okay. Just take it day by day."

~ Cynthia Harnisch-Breunig

Cynthia Harnisch-Breunig has worked extensively with high poverty children and adults. For thirteen years she was the President and CEO of Inner-City Arts, an oasis of learning, achievement, creativity and arts education located in the heart of Los Angeles' Skid Row. Honored as a Community Champion by the Annenberg Foundation, Cynthia is the president and CEO of Girl Scouts of San Gorgonio serving over 10,000 girls and 5,000 volunteers in Riverside and San Bernadino Counties.

www.inner-cityarts.org   *www.gssgc.org*

Dolores Huerta

Following My Heart

Do what you feel in your heart to be right — for you'll be criticized anyway. You'll be damned if you do and damned if you don't.

~ Eleanor Roosevelt

I was born in a small mining town in the mountains of northern New Mexico. My father was a farmer and mine worker by trade. After my parents divorced, my siblings and I moved with our mother to Stockton, California where we lived in a culturally diverse, but very poor, agricultural community of hard-working immigrant families.

My feminist seed was planted early on by my strong, independent, entrepreneur-mother. Known for her kindness and generosity, she was always an active participant in the community. My mother often said, "Never worry about what other people say about you as long as you know that what you are doing is the right thing."

In high school I was involved in numerous clubs and was active in Girl Scouts. Later, I earned a degree in education, got married, and became a teacher. Most of my students, like me, were from farm-worker families. It was very disturbing to see them coming to school with empty stomachs and bare feet.

When I went to the principal to discuss getting lunch vouchers for the poorest students, he said: "If their parents didn't drink their money away, they could afford to buy their kids lunch." This was not true! The farmers worked very hard for their wages, and they struggled to support their families. I was so angry that I decided to quit my job and help Cesar Chavez start a Farm Workers Union.

Knowing that my decision would be severely criticized, I went home and took a very long bath, so long that I had to heat and reheat the water many times over. "Here I am," I thought. "I have seven children. I'm a single mother going through a divorce. My family and I are living a comfortable middle-class life on my secure teacher's salary. Am I doing the right thing?" My heart said "yes."

That was the moment the storm of criticism began. "You are crazy! You will not succeed. You'll never be able to get another teaching job. Think about how this foolish decision will affect your children!" It wasn't until several years later, when the Farm Workers Union became a popular cause for celebrities across the entire country, that people began to apologize and appreciate what I had done.

In retrospect, starting the Farm Workers Union was the best decision I have ever made. Not only did I change lives, I was able to do something I truly loved. Even today, at the age of eighty-plus, people come up to me and say, "How can you keep doing what you do?" My answer is that I don't think about it. If you intellectualize all the reasons why you shouldn't do something, you will always find an excuse not to get started.

I believe society still tries to condition women to do what other people want us to do, and that is why a lot of women don't think they can make a difference. But the world will never change unless women claim their power, and in order to do that, we have to follow our hearts even if it means choosing the road less traveled at some point in our lives.

My advice to all women and girls is this: Don't be afraid of criticism! Have faith in your instincts, and do what you love—even if it sounds crazy to everyone else.

~ Dolores Huerta

Dolores Huerta, a tireless advocate for economic and social justice, is co-founder and First Vice President Emeritus of the United Farm Workers of America. She currently serves as President of the Dolores Huerta Foundation whose mission is to inspire, motivate and organize sustainable communities to attain social justice. She has received numerous awards including the Eleanor Roosevelt Human Rights Award. Six public schools are named after her and she has received and nine honorary Doctorate Degrees.

www.doloreshuerta.org

Deborah Hutchison

Driving My Destiny

If you obey all the rules, you miss all the fun.

~ Katharine Hepburn

My father never wavered in his demand for me to become a teacher. Ever since I can remember, he made it clear that teaching was my destiny. It didn't matter what dreams I may have had because my future was always set in stone—his.

In our household my father's alcohol came first and family second. Although Dad never physically harmed me, the verbal abuse was painful and the control suffocating. He was from the era of a three-martini lunch and a three-martini dinner. Not much time was left to nurture a child, but it was certainly enough to tear one down.

I was an average student in high school which was disappointing to a smart man who put himself through law school on the GI bill while working to feed his family. I was his big disappointment, and no matter how hard I tried to please him, it was never enough. That is why I always did exactly what he told me to do.

My father chose my college and dropped me off at campus telling me to get a teaching degree. I wasn't allowed to consider other possibilities. I didn't know there were any. Again I was the submissive, obedient daughter doing what my father instructed me to do.

Moving home after graduation was not an option. My father had given me an education, and I was expected to get a job. I was in for a shock—too many teachers and not enough positions. But Dad didn't care about my plight. "Just find a teaching job or get married" was his mantra. To financially exist, I took whatever job I could. I dreaded the weekly question, "Deborah, do you have a teaching job yet?"

Then an unexpected opportunity changed my life. A Hollywood movie company was coming to Chicago. A casting call for "extras" was advertised in the local papers. It paid very little, but I took the initiative and showed up to find hundreds of other people who had the same idea.

Standing in a long line, I met the casting director, filled out a form, had my picture taken and was sent home with "We'll call you if we need you." They did call me—and everyone else who showed up that day. I learned they would be shooting for one night, all night long. Totally thrilled, I didn't dare share my excitement with the family knowing how that discussion would end up.

One night of filming turned into three. Making friends with the crew, I learned that more movies were coming to Chicago. A floodgate of passion opened up when I had a sudden revelation. I didn't want to be a teacher! I could do anything I wanted to do—and drive my own destiny! That was the moment I decided to take charge of my life and not live by the rules that my father dictated. It was a bold, unfamiliar feeling, but something inside said to just take a leap. And what a leap it was!

Surely, Chicago needed to have its very own "extras" casting director. Who better to do it, than me? I was not trained, prepared or skilled for my new career, and I didn't know anyone who could help me. The only thing I knew was that I was in awe of the film-making process and had found my calling. So I decided to start my own casting company.

True to form, my father was not pleased with his first child's sudden streak of independence or her new choice of career. Pointing his finger at me, he shouted, "Being a casting director for Hollywood movies is the dumbest idea I ever heard! I sent you to college to be a teacher and, by God that is what you should be! What do you know about the movies anyway?" He did have a point. I really didn't know anything about the industry, but the more he derided me, the more determined I became to succeed.

If I wasn't working, my free time was spent putting the company together. Learning that another Hollywood movie was going to be filmed in Chicago, I thought "This is my chance!" I didn't get the job, but I was invited to stop by and watch the filming. Excited, I volunteered to help out wherever I could. Two weeks later, the production manager called with the break I'd been waiting for.

"Kid," he said, "I'm coming to Chicago for a re-shoot of some courtroom scenes. I need some sleazy lawyers—here's your chance to be Chicago's Extras Casting Director. Don't fail me!" Smiling, I picked up the telephone and called my father. "Hi Dad," I said. "We need a few lawyers to be in a movie I'm casting. I'd like to use you and some of the guys at the firm. What do you think?"

Dad and the other lawyers showed up for the shoot and had a blast! I never knew my father was such a ham. It was funny how he no longer seemed so intimidating. That was my first big break in the movie industry—an opportunity that led to the start of casting "extras" in thirty-five films and TV productions in Chicago for five years.

Then I sold my casting business, packed my bags and headed to the Golden State for the next step of my Hollywood adventure—just another gutsy gal proving that "If you obey all the rules, you miss all the fun!"

~ Deborah Hutchison

Deborah Hutchison is an Author, Filmmaker, Product Creator and Speaker. She is President/CEO of Gutsy Gals Inspire Me®, an inspirational media company promoting positive female role models by telling their stories. Gutsy Gals Inspire Me annually awards women/girls who are trail blazers, innovators and rule breakers. Deborah co-wrote the book "Put It in Writing!: Creating Agreements between Family and Friends" based on her agreements.

www.gutsygalsinspireme.com   *www.asaneapproach.com*

Monica Johnson

The Answer to a Prayer

There are … no coincidences. All events are blessings given to us to learn from.

~ Dr. Elizabeth Kubler-Ross

Twelve years ago, my husband lost his battle with cancer. Left with a business I didn't know how to run and a teenage daughter who depended on me to be strong, I descended into the lowest point of my life.

A friend suggested that I join a support group, and I agreed to attend a meeting. During the first session, I didn't say a word. I knew everyone else was in pain too, but I couldn't imagine how their grief compared to mine. I didn't go back until three years later. I became angry at everyone, including my husband for leaving me. How could God take him away so soon?

Business-wise, I didn't feel it was necessary to call customers or return their messages. Soon the phone grew silent. Late one afternoon it hit me—because the phone had stopped ringing, I wouldn't be able to pay any bills.

Wandering into the back yard, I cried out to my husband's spirit from the depths of my soul: "I need you now, right now! Help me to make a call! I can't do it on my own. You promised to be my guardian angel and look out for me and our daughter!"

I went back into the house and sat at my husband's desk. Glancing at his business rolodex, I let my fingers walk among his contacts. It was useless to think that anyone would be working this late on a Friday afternoon. Maybe I would try to make a call next week.

My fingers stopped on a random name. Without knowing what to say if someone should answer, I picked up the phone and dialed the number. To my surprise, a customer answered. "What a coincidence!" he said. "I was thinking of you this very moment, but I didn't want to call so late on a Friday evening. Do you have time to take an order?"

It was impossible for my customer to have known that my first business call was *not* a coincidence. It was the answer to a prayer.

~ Monica Johnson

Monica Johnson successfully assumed her late husband's position as partner and vice president in the Westape Co., and Seal Tape, Inc. She volunteers for many philanthropic organizations serving women and children in her local community including Las Madrecitas, Las Profesionales and the Palos Verdes Arts Center

www.sealtape.com

Linda Katz

Making Magic Happen

When it comes to saving the world or a part of it, street by street, neigh-
borhood by neighborhood, women are the catalysts through whom the
critical mass of social change will be achieved.

~ "Megatrends for Women"

My story about Dorothy, a chronically homeless African American woman known around town for her wild and crazy hair, is proof that you can't judge a book by its cover.

Her favorite dress was a bed sheet on which she drew a map of all the cities and states where she had ever lived. A transient living on the streets of San Diego when I met her almost twenty years ago, this very unusual woman never apologized for her peculiar appearance because that was simply who she was.

At the time I was serving on the board of Senior Community Centers, an organization dedicated to transforming the aging experience for seniors and helping them to live independently for as long as possible. I met Dorothy while working on a collaborative venture between the Senior Center and a local community theatre in Coronado.

The theatre invited our low-income, at-risk seniors to work with low-income, at-risk teenagers, one-on-one, during a summer program. The goal was to have seniors and teens get to know each other by writing and performing their own theatre reading at the end of the season. When Dorothy was asked to participate, she said that she needed to give it some thought.

A few days later Dorothy turned the invitation down saying, "They don't allow pedestrians on the bridge." After checking on the location, she realized that her lack of transportation would not allow her to get to the theatre without having the ability to walk across the Coronado Bridge. Once she was assured that the problem could be worked out, Dorothy agreed to participate in the program.

Imagine this curious looking transient homeless African American woman working with a sixteen year old teenage boy who had been abused for most of his life. In and out of foster care, he was hanging out with the wrong people and had become involved with drugs. Somehow, he ended up in the summer theatre program matched with Dorothy

This unlikely pair seemed to work well together, and they did a wonderful job performing at the end of the summer. Dorothy, of course, wore her favorite dress, and the audience roared with laughter when the teenage boy playfully said, "If you think there is no such thing as a bad hair day—then you haven't met Dorothy!"

A few years later I received a call from the director of the theatre who said she wanted to share a conversation that she had with the troubled teen—now a young man who had just graduated from community college. He was looking forward to his future and continuing his education! When the director asked what had happened to inspire him to turn his life around, he replied: "Dorothy."

The woman with the wild hair had a Masters Degree in Social Work until something caused her to end up homeless. Working in the summer theatre program with the troubled teenage boy, all her training and skills came rushing back. The young man explained that Dorothy had taken the time to really get to know and counsel him. It was her support and encouragement that pushed him forward.

In that moment I understood that Dorothy, a homeless woman, was, in fact, a generous philanthropist. She had given the best of herself to help heal the world. This realization deepened my awareness that individual contributions can't be measured by the same stick. One person may have dollars to give; another person may have time to share, and someone else can bring a unique talent to the table.

Dorothy escalated my appreciation for the differences among people. I made a conscious decision to always look for the best in every person and to surround myself with positive energy by working with organizations that reflect the rich diversity of my community.

One woman can indeed make a difference, but my personal philosophy is that "women can do more than woman." Like Dorothy, we each have a special gift to give, but I believe that when it comes to healing the world, working together is the key to making magic happen.

~ Linda Katz

Linda Katz, a co-founder of Women Give San Diego, has served as a community leader and activist for thirty years. She is Founding President of the San Diego Women's Foundation, a past board chair of Planned Parenthood of the Pacific Southwest, Senior Community Centers and Rady Children's Hospital Auxiliary. Linda has received numerous awards including San Diego Magazine's "Community Volunteer of the Year," Senior Community Center's Advocacy Hero Award and the Girl Scouts "Cool Woman" Award.

Kate Kendell

A Moment of Acceptance

*… the ideal should be to be capable of loving a woman or a man; either,
a human being, without feeling fear, restraint or obligation.*

~ Simone de Beauvoir, French philospher

I don't know why I thought it was a good idea to tell my mom that I was a lesbian while on a car ride to Portland, Oregon. I was twenty-two, and we were on a trip to visit my grandparents, other family members, and a man that she was dating. I had been involved with my then-girlfriend for over six months, and it was getting harder to portray us as just roommates and friends.

My parents were divorced, and Mom and I were especially close during this time. Since we only lived a few miles away from each other, I saw her at least once a week. I was excited about our road trip, but worried about how my devout Mormon mother, whom I loved deeply and very much needed in my life, might react to the news that I was gay.

The worst-case scenario would be that she would burst into angry tears and say that I was a huge disappointment. The best thing that could happen, and the reaction I most expected, was hearing mom say that she was not happy about my sexual orientation, but she still loved me and that together we would find a way to make it work.

We left bright and early on a crisp spring day. The reality of what I was about to tell my mother hung over me like a dark cloud. We were in the car for about an hour when I just couldn't hold it in any longer. "Mom," I began, "I need to tell you something, but I'm not sure how you will react. I'm really scared." "Honey," Mom responded, "I hope you know that you can tell me anything."

Finally, I just blurted it out,"Mom, I'm gay."

There was complete silence for a second or two, and my heart seemed to freeze mid-beat. Then my mother reached over and took my hand. "Honey," she said, as she looked me in the eye, tears welling up, "The only thing that matters to me is that you are happy." I felt a flood of joy and relief! The rest of the road trip was spent answering all her questions. When did I know? What was this part of my life, the part that she wasn't aware of, like?

The knowledge that I had my mother's ongoing love and respect made it easier to believe in myself and to trust. I took more chances, embraced new opportunities, and came to believe that anything is possible. Until the day she died, my mother was always my steadfast champion. I will never forget that moment of unabashed and unconditional acceptance. It has made the rest of my very fulfilled life possible.

~ Kate Kendell

Kate Kendell is the Executive Director for the National Center for Lesbian Rights, a legal organization that fights for the civil and human rights of lesbian, gay, bisexual and transgender people and their families through litigation, public policy and education. Kate was named "a woman who could be president" by the San Francisco League of Women Voters and a hero of GLBT History Month. In 2004 she was selected as one of California's Top 100 Attorneys.

www.nclr.org

Nancy D. Kimber, MD

Breaking the Silence

Until we have the courage to recognize cruelty for what it is ... whether its victim is human or animal ...we cannot expect things to be much better in this world...

~ Rachel Carson, American marine biologist

Every year I volunteer at a sanctuary for abused animals. On one particular day, I asked to see the pit bulls that had been recently rescued from a notorious illegal dog-fighting ring. A trainer said they were not available for volunteers to work with, but after a long conversation, he agreed to show me a dog named Georgia.

"Oh My God!" I thought when I saw the look of hopelessness and despair in her eyes. "This is the epitome of a battered woman!" The trainer explained that she had been used to breed multiple litters of pit bulls destined for cruelty and trained to fight. Before being rescued, Georgia had given birth to over fifty pups! When she could no longer breed, she would become the next bait dog. I was horrified to learn that her teeth were removed so she wouldn't be able to defend herself!

That was the moment the light bulb went on. I had never considered that the psychology behind animal abuse and violence against women is very similar—so the batterer can control his victim—and completely annihilate her spirit. As a physician specializing in women's reproductive health, it struck me that I was in the perfect position to educate my patients about the shocking realities of gender-violence in the United States.

One in four American women is exposed to intimate-partner violence at least once in her life; three are killed by their partners every day. Intimate-partner violence is the leading cause of female injuries in this country, and nearly five million women are assaulted or raped by their partners every year. In spite of these staggering statistics, less than twenty-percent of battered females seek the medical treatment they need.

Hear me loud and clear: it is absolutely never okay to ever accept any kind of physical, sexual or mental abuse from another human being under any circumstance. If you are being abused, come forward and break the silence. You are not alone.

If you know someone who is a victim of abuse, please be a good friend. Help her to get medical attention and professional support. We must all do our part to ensure that every human being, and every living creature, is treated with dignity, kindness and respect.

~ Nancy D. Kimber, MD, F.A.C.O.G

Dr. Nancy Kimber is a licensed American Board of Obstetrics & Gynecology certified physician in private practice with a strong focus on women and children. She was honored as the "Child Advocate of the Year" by the End Abuse Council of Long Beach, a multi-disciplinary group of domestic violence and child abuse agencies. A reserve police officer for the City of Long Beach, Nancy is the sexual assault consultant for the Long Beach Police Department and medical advisor to Forensic Nurse Specialists.

www.nancykimbermd.com

Irene L. Kinoshita

Outside My Comfort Zone

Fear is only as deep as the mind allows.

~ Japanese Proverb

There weren't many Japanese-Americans living in Ogden, Utah after World War II, and my yellow skin didn't fit in with the predominantly white culture. Cast out of the main, my mother would say, "Don't do anything to embarrass yourself or the family." Girls were expected to stay close to home, get married, and have lots of children. It was unthinkable that any woman, especially an Asian female, could run a business on her own.

When I became an entrepreneur many years later, I loved the challenges of starting a new technology company with my two male partners. The team worked tirelessly to meet payroll and pay the bills. At least that's what I thought. I soon learned that the president, who had a proven record with start-up ventures, was using profits to fund his personal software business while our company was barely squeaking out payroll!

Since I had guaranteed credit lines and leases on the buildings, I was placed on credit hold. Product shipments came to a screeching halt; unable to ship product, the company was headed for failure. Knowing that my trust was violated by someone I had considered to be an honest business partner made the whole situation even more devastating.

My reputation was at stake. Our employees and their families depended upon me. Unable to eat or sleep, cash flow and inventory concerns formed an invisible noose around my neck. Building and managing the sales force was my primary responsibility, but as majority investor I had the power to take over the company and declare myself president. However, leading the company through a major crisis was never part of my business plan.

It was easy to convince myself that I didn't possess the skills to pull the company through this disastrous turn of events. After all, there were four strikes against me: I was a woman. I was a minority. I was in a male-dominated technology industry, and I didn't have any experience running a business. I just wanted to stay inside my comfort zone where it felt safe and familiar.

What if I failed? It was hard to push through the fear of embarrassing myself, but I knew I had to try. Mustering up all my courage, I appointed myself president of the company, wrested control, and ousted the former president through a series of legal strategies. From that moment on, there was no going back.

My concerns about being a minority woman heading a business in a male-dominated field were unwarranted. Many supportive people came forward to help me succeed. The company thrived under my leadership, and I began to see every challenge as another opportunity to grow. With this new attitude, one year later I was proud to say that I had started a business, taken it over, and turned it around successfully!

If I can step outside my comfort zone, you can too. Never let the fear of embarrassing yourself stand in the way of your own success.

~ Irene L. Kinoshita

Irene Kinoshita is co-founder, president & chief executive officer of Ascolta Training Company, a leading provider of information technology training and learning services. She is the recipient of many awards and honors including The American Red Cross Clara Barton Award for Outstanding Women, the Elizabeth Dole Glass Ceiling Award, and the Women Business Owner of the Year Award.

www.ascolta.com

Brooke Knapp

Flying Solo

The most difficult thing is the decision to act, the rest is merely tenacity.
The fears are paper tigers. You can do anything you decide to do. You
can act to change and control your life ...the process is its own reward.

~ Amelia Earhart

My mother was a great woman who always said that I could do anything if I put my mind to it, but there was a time in my life when I didn't believe her. In my early twenties I was fearful of almost everything. Nothing I did was ever good enough.

Although I graduated college with honors, my male friends were getting job offers in the brokerage business, but companies weren't accepting my applications. Looking back, this was probably the root of my lack of self-confidence. I had to attend secretarial school and learn how to type and take shorthand in order to get hired.

Then I began to realize that my fears were holding me back from living a wonderful life. I knew many successful people who were taking risks, and as a result they were learning and growing and accomplishing exciting things. So I decided to create a little game for myself and called it "No Guts, No Glory."

The first step in the game was to make a list and prioritize everything that terrified me. Even though I was surrounded by aviation enthusiasts, including my husband, the fear of flying was number one on the list. Airplanes scared me to death! Every weekend I would go the airport hangar and watch my husband and his friends take off in their bi-planes and war-birds while I stayed behind and waited for them to return.

Determined to conquer my number one fear, I signed up for flying lessons telling myself that I could always cancel. I showed up for class about 50% of the time, and when I did, I was at least 45 minutes late. The instructor said I was the only student he ever had who enjoyed ground school more than flying. Gradually, I mustered up the courage to board a plane. I literally had to force myself to look at the instruments in the cockpit.

In order to get my pilots' license, I had to fly solo in a triangle consisting of 3 legs, 100 miles apiece. My chosen route was from Santa Monica airport to Porterville to Santa Maria and back to Santa Monica. Average people solo in 17 hours; it took me 60 hours.

When my plane lifted off the ground and flew over the wilderness area in the mountains north of the San Fernando Valley, I was trembling so hard that I could barely breathe. The experience of being in the air all alone became so overwhelming that I made a left turn and landed in Camarillo where I called my husband and cried, "I can't do it! I'm not meant to be a pilot!" In his loving and understanding way he said, "You gutless coward! Get back in the plane and fly to Porterville."

So I got back in my plane with tears streaming downing my face. When I landed in Porterville, I jumped out of the plane and kissed the ground. Then, rushing up to the first person I saw, I said "Please sign my log book! My husband and friends will never believe that I made it here all on my own!"

After filling the plane with fuel, I took off to Santa Maria. About an hour later I was hooked. I was flying solo and I loved it! It was fun! It was exhilarating! My mother was right! I could do anything if I put my mind to it. The sudden awareness that I was a perfectly capable young woman took me by surprise. From that moment on, my mother's words became the basis for the rest of my life.

My greatest fear evolved into my greatest passion, and I wanted more than to just be accepted by my aviation peers. I wanted to be respected. I went on to set or break over 100 world aviation speed records including the fastest speed around the world in a civilian jet aircraft. Overcoming my number one fear not only broadened my entire outlook on life, it created many exciting opportunities that I never would have had.

Identifying fears and making a plan to overcome them is still a part of my life. The process itself can be a huge learning experience if only in the trying. It really doesn't matter what a particular fear is. You can do it. Just remember—"No Guts, No Glory!"

~ Brooke Knapp

Brooke Knapp is a renowned aviator, entrepreneur and realtor. She received the Federal Aviation Award for extraordinary service after her 1984 "Flight for World's Children" flew through the People's Republic of China and the Soviet Union delivering letters of peace and friendship from children in the U.S raising over $1,000,000 for UNICEF. Previously, she founded and operated Jet Airways, Inc. Currently, Brooke is a licensed realtor with Sotheby's International Realty in Beverly Hills.

Catherine Lamberti

The Joy of Serving

Service is the rent we pay for being. It is the very purpose of life, and not something that you do in your spare time.

~ Marian Wright Edelman, founder
Children's Defense Fund

I was a twenty-three-year-old white teacher walking into a prefabricated classroom without air conditioning in South Africa on a blistering hot summer day. The energy in the room immediately frightened me! I asked my students, thirty black tenth-grade young men between the ages of eighteen and twenty, what was going on—but no one answered.

Something was very wrong. Shutting the door and windows, I said, "Now you can speak freely. Whatever we discuss here today will not go anywhere." A wave of fear swept over me when someone mumbled, "We are going to burn down the school."

Growing up in a privileged white community in the 1970s, I didn't really understand the pain of apartheid, a government sponsored system of legal racial segregation that sparked violent civil unrest throughout South Africa between 1948 and 1990. "Okay," I said, "Tell me why you want to burn down the school."

An angry student stood up and threw his books at me. "Look at these marks," he shouted. "100%! 85%! 90%! 95%! What does it matter? I'm black!" "Yeah! Yeah! We're black! We're black!" the rest of the class agreed. "What does it matter?"

I quickly realized what would happen if my students carried out their plan. A terrible riot would occur during which I and the other two white teachers would be murdered in a brutal method called necklacing. A car tire would be placed over my shoulders and arms, and a gallon of gasoline would be poured on my body. Then someone would light a match and set me on fire! That was the way enraged black students dealt with white teachers during an apartheid riot. It had been happening all over the country.

I don't remember if there was any physical movement on my part, but I felt my spirit fall back inside myself as I flashed on what I knew was coming. From the depths of my soul I prayed, "God help me"—and in that moment of absolute terror, I tapped into a source of divine inspiration that saved my life.

Calmly, I walked to the front of the room with my arms at my side and said, "If I was black, I would want to do what you want to do. I have never understood how painful it is to be black in this country, and I am so sorry. But let's look at our options.

"There is a military barrack ten minutes away. If you start to riot, one of three things will happen: the military will arrive, and some of you will die. Some of you will go to jail, and some of you will run into the hills. But all of you will have lost your school. Think with me. Maybe there's a fourth option."

There was a lot of grumbling. I had caught their attention and needed to keep talking. "Apartheid," I continued, "will not last. The day is coming when it will be over. Where will you be when apartheid ends? Will you be in jail as a convicted felon? Living in the hills without an education? Will you be dead? Or will you be highly educated and ready to take the lead when our country needs strong black leaders?"

The room became silent. Reminding the students that they would be writing an exam in three months as part of a national test for tenth graders across South Africa, I said, "Let's make a contract. If you decide to be highly educated, I promise that as hard as you work, I will work harder. I will be there every step of the way to make sure you get the marks that you deserve." The students accepted the contract, and I walked around the room shaking hands with each one. Then we set to work.

When the test results came in at 92%, the senior teacher said my marks were too high and told me to lower them by 20% because the national board would reject them as lenient. No way! I made a commitment to my students! These marks were earned! Digging in my heels and refusing to back down, an independent evaluator was flown in from another part of the country. After reviewing my students' work, he said I was strict, not lenient. He fully endorsed the marks!

Looking back, I could have been killed in a terrible way. Putting aside my self-centered view of the world and crossing over into the hearts and souls of my students is what saved my life. But in helping them to deal with their pain, I learned about the joy of serving others and realized there is no other way to live.

~ Catherine Lamberti

Catherine Lamberti, Chief Executive Officer of Exercise Technology Inc., is the inventor of the Sportswall play-based fitness technology and is the driving force behind the company's infrastructure, product concept, design and development in thirty-two countries. She has twenty-five years of international entrepreneurial experience creating and selling successful companies and is a recipient of the 2011 National Association of Women Business Owners' Spirit of Entrepreneurship Award in Santa Barbara.

www.xergames.com

Betty LaMarr

Becoming Fearless

Fear stops you in your tracks. Self-confidence propels you forward.

~ Unknown

One of the biggest risks I have ever taken was making the decision to leave a successful career in corporate America and accept a job abroad. I was in my mid-forties, recently divorced, and my son had completed his education. For the first time, I only had to think about my needs, and I found myself yearning for a more meaningful work life.

Climbing the ladder and earning a big paycheck weren't important anymore. I had played the game long enough to know that doing more of the same would not bring happiness. I started to wonder: What do I want my legacy to be? Do I want to live the rest of my life thinking, "I really wish that I had," or "I'm really glad that I did?"

During this time of introspection, a little voice relentlessly attempted to instill fear in me, saying: "What if things don't work out for you in a foreign country? You'll need to start over! Corporations won't value your skills when you return!" Then one day I realized the little voice of fear was only trying to protect a perceived lifestyle of a "good job and good money" and what I thought was respect from other people.

I decided to make the big leap and just go for it. I would face my fear, take a cut in pay and free myself from an attachment to material things and "stuff." That was the moment I gave myself permission to experience life fully and completely instead of merely being a spectator. I packed my bags and moved to South Africa!

When I arrived, a contagious feeling of hope was in the air. A new president had just been elected in the country's first free elections. I was given opportunities that I never could have dreamed of having in the United States, like being invited to functions at the American Ambassador's home and attending the coronation of a King. I was recognized as an American, not as a hyphenated African-American. My professional experience was valued, and people listened intently to what I had to say.

Privileged to be part of the best of times, I felt a sense of responsibility to help remedy the worst of times for people who were not as fortunate. I started to understand the difference between my wants and needs and appreciated how much less I needed to be truly satisfied. As a result, I became more confident in my skills and abilities instead of relying on material things for approval.

I knew that if I had stayed in my corporate cocoon, I would have missed the opportunity to meet people from all over the world, people with Ivy League educations who had given up Wall Street jobs to work for the good of humanity. I might never have learned the lesson of Ubuntu, an African philosophy that affirms the dignity of every human being because, in spite of our differences, "We are One."

"A person with Ubuntu is open and available to others," Archbishop Desmond Tutu writes, "... does not feel threatened that others are able and good, for he or she has a proper self-assurance that comes from knowing that he or she belongs in a greater whole and is diminished when others are diminished or humiliated, when others are tortured or oppressed." When you have the quality of Ubuntu, you serve the community, and you are known for your kindness and generosity.

When I left South Africa four amazing years later, I was filled with gratitude for the opportunity to have lived and worked in such a special place. I had learned to connect with my own values and with the "what" of life knowing that the "how" will always reveal itself in due time. I had become fearless instead of fearful!

~ Betty LaMarr

Betty LaMarr is the Executive Director of the EmpowHer Institute, a nonprofit organization that she founded upon returning from South Africa in 2003. EmpowHer supports low and moderate income females to develop entrepreneurship as a career option and encourages lifelong learning while developing a meaningful and satisfying lifestyle. Betty has been honored as one of Los Angeles County's "Women Who Make a Difference."

www.empowher.org

Artis Lane

Breakthrough

Memories of our lives, of our work and our deeds will continue in others.

~ Rosa Parks

At the age of five, mesmerized by butterflies pollinating a field of wildflowers, I lacked the words to express my connection to God. I was an old soul, never a child. "Just rise above it," I would say as a teenager when people asked me for advice, "like you are looking down on your life. Then you can be objective and know how to guide it. You are one with your wisdom whose source is God."

Looking back over my eighty-some years as an artist, my "emerging out of matter into spirit" concept was my biggest epiphany. My motivation to sculpt and paint prominent personalities or express social injustice, for example, *The Beginning*, a painting of Rosa Parks on the bus, and *Sojourner Truth*, a bust of an African American woman on display in the U.S. Capitol, was superseded by the urge to go to an even higher level with my work.

One day, at the foundry to oversee the completion of a bronze head of a woman, I was able to view the piece in mid-process. After the bronze had been poured and set, the outer ceramic shell holding the wax mold in place was removed. Instead of seeing a beautifully polished finished product, I saw a half-finished piece with glistening bronze peering out from behind chunks of chalky ceramic shell and coiled wire.

To me, this was the exact visual metaphor for the process by which we move out of the physical world and into the realm of perfected thought! Covered in "birthing material," the bronze head represented human imperfection. In her one visible eye I saw a soul yearning for Truth. Chunks of the ceramic shell on her head symbolized the human experience of breaking out of matter into spirit.

I am recognized as the first artist to understand and utilize the expressive and symbolic potential of leaving the "accidents" of the bronzing process on a finished piece. From my perspective this is what makes the technique part of Divine Creation, almost as if the fragmenting process is designing itself. Of course, I make artistic decisions at every turn, deciding if a fragment is right or not. It is always a surprise to discover how the ceramic mold left behind, and the finished bronze peering through, interact with each other.

The birth of my "emerging out of matter into spirit" concept is my most transformative moment. I could use the bronze head of the woman, which I later called "Breakthrough" with all the generic man pieces, to portray man rising out of the darkness and into the Truth of his being—the enlightened Truth of man created in God's image, as opposed to God in man's image.

~ Artis Lane

Artis Lane is an African-American artist who was born in North Buxton, Ontario, Canada. A renowned, award-winning painter and sculptor, she works on three levels of consciousness: Portraiture, Social Justice and Divine Metaphysics. Her work is grounded in what she sees as enduring spiritual truths that connect all humanity to a universal force. As an artist, her goal is for her work to uplift and inspire viewers to find perfection in their own being.

www.artislane.com

Ellen Lapham

Born to Climb

…climbing is a form of exploration that inspires me to confront my own inner nature within nature. …This intuitive state of being is what allows me to experience moments of true freedom and harmony.

~ Lynn Hill

I've always known that I was born to climb. As a little child, I loved to climb anything vertical including stairs and trees. Growing up in the flat Midwest, there weren't any big hills. No one in my family had ever climbed a mountain. Still, a passion for climbing was inside of me from the get-go, and I was always looking up to see how high I could reach.

One cold wintry night, during the lowest point in my life, I slept in an ice cave on a shoulder of the highest mountain in the world. My business was not where I wanted it to be; as a mother I felt estranged from my son during his teenage years, and I was grieving the loss of both my parents. Filled with self-doubt, I wondered if there was anything that I could do well.

People said I was crazy to join an expedition to put the first American woman on the summit of Mount Everest. In some ways, they were right. I had climbed mountains in Asia before, but never anything as high and as dangerous as a Fall season climb on the North side. This was not a "guided" climb, so I had to be self-reliant and really know what I was doing. But it was exciting to think that I could play a role in proving to the world that an American woman could take on something as big as Everest and succeed.

Climbing up the west ridge of Mount Everest earlier that day was particularly challenging due to the high altitude, low oxygen, and ferocious winds. My throat hurt, my eyes burned, and every muscle in my body ached from carrying my 40-pound pack. After taking a few steps forward, my five-foot-two-and-a-half inch frame was repeatedly slammed to the ground. At seven thousand meters (23,000 feet) my Sherpa teammates decided to return to base camp, but I was too worn out to take another step. So, I decided to spend the night alone and return in the morning.

Outside the cave, the wind was howling and snow was falling. Inside, I struggled to stay warm and got up every hour to make sure the entrance tunnel was still open. It's possible to suffocate in an ice cave blocked by snow. At sunrise I awoke to a spectacular heart-stopping view of northern Tibet's snow-covered mountain peaks and the snaky Rongbuk Glacier way below. I remember feeling so serene, proud that I had actually done something quite remarkable! What I didn't know was that the true test of my ability was only a moment away.

Making radio contact with base camp, I learned that a blizzard was headed in our direction. I packed my gear and started down the mountain, but in a matter of minutes, I was in a total whiteout. I tried to stay on the route we had taken on the way up, but even the most experienced climbers can get lost and become disoriented in a blinding snowstorm.

Descending Mount Everest proved to be harder than climbing up, and without my team, I had to totally rely on myself. I had no idea if I could even make it to base camp alive. But something inside pushed me forward saying, "Stay calm and focused. Give it everything you've got. You have pulled through difficult situations before." It suddenly hit me that life had been preparing me for this daunting challenge for a very long time.

I knew there were deep crevasses underneath the snow, and in the blink of an eye, I could disappear without a trace. I thought about a particular saying among climbers—"The Mountain will decide." The only thing I could do was just put one foot in front of the other, step by step. Ten hours later, nearly frozen to death, I reached the safety of base camp—all on my own!

For me, climbing has always been less a public performance and more of an internal endeavor. But now I can see that I learned more about myself on the way down the mountain than I ever learned climbing up. I didn't really have a choice that day, and I did what I had to do, but succeeding on my own in the face of tremendous adversity gave me my self-confidence back!

I realized that success isn't always about how high you can go. Sometimes, it's having the courage to just stay calm and focused during the dark hours of life, putting your best foot forward and giving it everything you've got—one little step at a time. There will always be days when it's enough to just wake up and show up! No one can stand on the top of a summit for very long before having to come back down to reality again.

Climbing will always be one of my greatest passions, and I'll never stop trying to reach as high as I possibly can. After all, there will always be another mountain to conquer in the remarkable journey that is life.

~ Ellen Lapham

Ellen Lapham is a Silicon Valley serial entrepreneur and turn-around CEO for high tech, high goal companies. Her executive coaching helps entrepreneurial women overcome roadblocks to success. Her community work focuses on two themes: the mountain environment and the status of women. Ellen is a member of the International Women's Forum and was a C-200 Foundation director. A director of the American Alpine Club, in 2011 she co-led a scientific expedition to Peru's high Cordillera Blanca.

www.aimhigh1.com

Dorothy Largay

When the Wall Came Down

It is this belief in a power larger than myself and other than myself which allows me to venture into the unknown and even the unknowable

~ Maya Angelou

The most exhilarating experience of my life was when the Berlin Wall came down. I had the privilege of being one of the first Americans to walk through the Brandenburg Gate on the day that East Germany was reunited with the West. It was a coincidence that I was in Berlin during this monumental historical occasion. A business trip had been planned months in advance. No one had any idea that it would occur during the reunification of Germany!

It was amazing to see so many people in one place milling around and experiencing freedom for the first time. Families and friends joined together in euphoric celebration. Children, wide-eyed with wonder, didn't know what to think. Young couples tentatively walked across the plaza, hand-in-hand in quiet conversation as if saying, "What is our future? Anything is possible now. We are free! But what does freedom really mean?" Excitement met trepidation. Isn't that what opportunity offers?

I knew what was happening in Berlin would affect the United States. It was a dramatic event for the entire world! I also realized that it was affecting me on a very deep and personal level. I was more than an eyewitness to history-in-the-making when the wall came down. In a foreign country, thousands of miles from home, I was struck by the awareness that I was part of something much bigger.

It's hard to explain exactly how this sudden feeling came about, but it brought me to the conclusion that we are all in this together. I was filled with the excitement of knowing that I had the potential to really make a difference in the world. I quit my job and decided to venture out on my own.

The next step was finding partners to help me consult with professionals in Eastern Europe and teach them how to manage their businesses in the new market economy. Having the guts to take on a risk this big was something I never would have previously considered. But one evening seven years earlier, the coroner knocked on my door. My husband had been in a terrible car accident and was killed by a drunk driver.

My beloved husband was a brilliant man and a real maverick in the sense of being innovative, intuitive, creative, and a fiercely independent thinker. Soulmates and best friends, I never doubted for a minute that he loved me unconditionally. Devastated, my only peace was in knowing there were no regrets. In retrospect, what I loved in him most was what I was able to become after he died.

Growing up in a conservative community in New England and educated in a small Catholic convent school, I had led a very sheltered life. Before I met my husband, professionally I was rather timid, but after he died, that quickly changed. When the most important thing in my world was gone, there was nothing left for me to fear. I became someone with a lot more guts, a woman who could take risks and break out of the conventional shell.

What I experienced in Berlin was a rare moment of personal awakening. We are in this together. We are connected. Everyone is part of the whole. This awareness helped me to conquer my fears, to develop my skills and take risks.

When a woman uses her voice, she uses it to provide for the ones she loves and to invest in her community. Helping underserved women in developing countries has become my passion. Helping them helps me. Bettering their world betters mine. We are connected. Isn't it exhilarating to know that we are part of something bigger than ourselves?

~ Dorothy Largay

Dorothy Largay is the founder of the Linked Foundation, a private foundation that promotes and invests in high impact solutions to alleviate poverty in Latin American and the U.S. with a focus on economic self-reliance and healthcare for women. Previously, she was the Executive Director at Santa Clara University's Executive Development Center and the Director of Worldwide Leadership Development at Apple, Inc. Dorothy served as Chairman of the Board of Direct Relief International 2009-2011.

www.linkedfoundation.org

Kimi Lee

A Moment of Clarity

… Finding out who you are is not simple. It takes a lot of hard work and courage to get to know who you are and what you want.

~ Sue Bender, author

At the age of twenty-five, I didn't have a clue about who I really was. I didn't know what I wanted to do with my life, and I didn't know where I wanted to go. One night, feeling as if my entire world was crashing around me, I sat in my car alone and cried.

It wasn't about any one thing. It was everything. I had moved three hundred miles away from my very close-knit family and friends and was working in a place that I did not want to be at. Sleeping on a friend's couch for three months, I couldn't find the perfect job and yet another dating relationship had come to an end. My life was in chaos.

When I graduated from college three years earlier, I became the director of a state-wide nonprofit organization, a job I wasn't ready for, but I accepted the challenge and ran it successfully. Then wanting to venture out on my own and try something new, everything fell apart. Crying in the car, it was hard to admit that I didn't know myself at all.

I thought about my parents who had fled Burma when the military dictatorship started to rid ethnic Chinese from the country and how they ended up in San Francisco where I was born and raised. My mother worked as seamstress in the garment industry to make ends meet. When I was a child, she showed me a dress and said, "This sells for two-hundred dollars. I was paid two dollars to make it." I didn't understand the significance of her remark at the time but it stayed with me.

I began to get clarity about the fact that I was fortunate to have the opportunity to do whatever I wanted with my life. I just needed to decide what that was and then figure out how to make it happen. Then the truth hit me like a ton of bricks—I was actually very insecure and lacked confidence in myself.

That's when I understood how every poor decision I had ever made was connected to this moment of feeling miserable and alone. My sorry state of mind was all about not being able to be happy because I didn't know who I was. I realized the perfect career or the perfect relationship was never going to fall out of the sky and land in my lap.

I found a job in a large national organization that exposed me to many different people and points of view. This choice helped me to break through my tiny bubble and really think about where I could best fit in the larger world. Soon I discovered an opportunity that connected all the pieces of my life—to help build a nonprofit organization that would assist low-wage workers in the garment industry. Once I found my niche, everything else in my life came together.

Today I am a happily married mother of two wonderful children. Reflecting upon the various choices I made in my twenties, I have come to understand that each decision I make going forward will affect the well-being of my family, my health, and my career.

A woman's mind, body and spirit are all connected. It's impossible to put our best thoughts out into the world, and do the work that we are meant to do, until we discover who we really are.

~ Kimi Lee

Kimi Lee was honored as part of Lifetime's award-winning "Every Woman Counts" campaign spotlighting extraordinary women. She is a senior fellow at the Movement Strategy Center supporting individuals, organizations, alliances and sectors to be more strategic, collaborative and sustainable, and the Lead Organizer for the Excluded Workers Congress, a network of national worker alliances. Founder and former director of the Garment Workers Center in Los Angeles, Kimi now sits on the board of directors.

www.movementstrategy.org

Tilly Levine

Moving Forward

Life is not the way it's supposed to be. It's the way it is. The way you deal with it is what makes the difference.

~ Virginia Satir, author

I was born in Israel where mandatory service in the Israeli army is required for both men and women. There, at the age of nineteen, I met my husband-to-be. It was love at first sight! We were best friends and soul mates, and I believed with all my heart that our romance would last forever.

We married and traveled to the United States wanting to experience everything it had to offer. On a journey for adventure, we found freedom. We decided to stay in America and begin our life together in a new world where we could create our own destiny.

It wasn't easy. We lived in a humble one-room apartment. I cleaned houses, worked as a driver and a clerk in a jewelry store. We sold toys and clothing at a local swap meet on weekends, but all that mattered was that we had each other. Eventually, we became proud parents of two beautiful daughters and started a clothing company that would bring us great prosperity and success.

Then, somehow, passion waned and our romance ended. We tried our best, but the marriage could not be saved. We had grown into different people with different needs. My entire world fell apart, and I now had to accept my new identity as a divorced woman and single mother. Disillusioned, angry and confused, I still had to work side-by-side with my former husband everyday and help grow the business as if nothing was wrong.

After many months of sadness, my sense of survival kicked in, and I realized that I had a choice: I could let go of my marriage and look toward the future. Or I could hold on to the past and remain angry and unhappy. In that moment I decided to forgive my ex-husband and myself for all that went wrong and move forward in a spirit of friendship and respect for the father of my children. Once I made that decision, I never looked back.

In the process I discovered one of life's greatest gifts: emotional freedom. I can't always control what happens around me, but I have the ability to control what happens inside me. I hold the key to open or close my heart. I am responsible for creating my destiny.

My ex-husband and I have remained business partners and best friends working side-by-side creating and building the brand of successful stores that bear my name. I have since remarried and am proud that our two families have merged in a spirit of camaraderie, admiration and love. Life doesn't always turn out the way we expect, but with forgiveness and a positive attitude, we can still move forward and achieve our dreams.

~ Tilly Levine

Tilly Levine is co-founder of Tilly's a fast-growing specialty youth retailer since 1982. Tilly has been an advocate to help disadvantaged youth through her support of mentoring programs, youth shelters and educational initiatives. She founded Tilly's Baby Home, an innovative approach to maintaining unity in a family-style environment caring for newborns and infants who are removed from their home. Tilly's dream is to establish a life center that will empower youth with hope and positive energy.

www.tillys.com

Lori Leyden

A Moment of Grace

Grace fills empty spaces, but it can only enter where there is a void to receive it, and it is Grace itself, which makes this void.

~ Simone Weil

A devoutly religious child, at the age of twelve I turned to my parish priest for spiritual guidance. Vulnerable and confused, I reached out to a man who I truly believed was God's representative on earth only to become a victim of sexual abuse.

The abuse occurred during a particularly difficult time in my life. My mom, suffering from an undiagnosed depression since the death of her mother, had fallen ill and was unable to nurture her five children. My father, a policeman, worked three jobs to support our family and was rarely home. As the oldest, I was suddenly responsible for three younger siblings, plus a newborn. I could not have imagined how my childhood experiences would connect me with my life's purpose in such a profound way.

Years later, meditating about what lay ahead, I asked to know the next step in my spiritual journey. Soon the answer arrived via an email from a woman I had never met. The woman explained that she worked with survivors of the Rwandan genocide and found meditation and relaxation exercises to be very healing for these women and orphans. After reading my stress management handbook, she was writing to ask if I would agree to have portions of my work translated into Kinyarwanda, the native language of Rwanda.

We agreed to meet, and I instantly knew this was much more than just a casual encounter. It was the next step on my soul adventure, an adventure that would take me across the world and into the depths of my own heart. In the fall of 2007 I traveled to Rwanda to teach trauma healing skills to men, women and children who had survived one of the worst human-inflicted tragedies of our time.

Horrific descriptions of mutilation, ethnic cleansing and rape broke my heart open, and the stories of the orphan-heads-of-households called to my soul. After enduring their own torture and abuse, hundreds of thousands of young trauma survivors were forced to witness their parents' murders. Then they were left to care for up to six other younger orphans without food, shelter, clothing or any visible means of support.

During my first trauma healing session with a group of about one hundred orphan-heads-of-households, I offered my deepest apology for what had happened in their country and acknowledged the horrors they had lived through. I shared the sorrow of my own childhood, and even though their traumas were so much more extreme than my own, we bonded in shared compassion for each other. I quickly realized these courageous young survivors were my inspiring teachers as well as my students.

As we engaged in our healing journey together, I could feel the resonance of love and connectedness in the room growing and expanding. Time seemed to stand still, and I began to experience a transcendent state of Oneness, synchronicity and awareness. Suddenly everything that had happened in my life started to make sense. My journey to Rwanda was as much about receiving as it was about giving!

In that Moment of Grace it became clear that the abuse and circumstances of my childhood served a far greater purpose. In Grace, our ego and sense of separation dissolve into a resonance of harmony, peace and Oneness with our Divinity. I knew that I had been brought to Rwanda to discover my life's work.

~ Lori Leyden

Lori Leyden, Ph.D., MBA, is the author of the "Stress Management Handbook: Strategies for Health and Inner Peace" and creator of the Grace Process, a spiritual practice for heart-centered living. Upon returning from Rwanda, she founded Create Global Healing, a nonprofit organization committed to heart-opening experiences for orphans in war-torn countries, U.S. students, humanitarians and philanthropists. Lori's latest project is Project Light, the first international youth healing, leadership and job development program.

www.createglobalhealing.org   *www.projectlightrwanda.org*

Carol Liu

The Art of Politics

The challenge is to practice politics as the art of making what appears to be impossible, possible.

~ Hillary Clinton

Before I entered politics, two experiences captured my need to help create a better world.

The first occurred in the late 1960s when I was student-teaching seniors in American Government at Richmond High School in Richmond, California. The class was diverse economically, socially and racially. As part of their studies, I made arrangements to take them on a field trip to visit a museum in San Francisco.

My memorable learning experience: for the majority of students on the bus, it was the first time they had ever crossed the Bay Bridge or been in San Francisco! How can that be? What is the relationship between poverty and opportunity? How do you ensure an equal playing field for all? Shouldn't everyone have a chance to reach their potential?

The second experience was when I read a book, titled *Rashomon*, a Japanese crime mystery about several individuals who witness a murder in a park. When interviewed by authorities, each person had a similar, but different version of what had occurred. How can that be? Why are the witness's stories so different from one another?

The field trip focused my life on trying to ensure that every American has a quality education. Education is a critical part of self-esteem, self-sufficiency and good citizenship—and hopefully, better communities. *Rashomon* helped me understand that "truth" is in the eye of the beholder. There are many "truths" to every event. Every voice is important, and listening to every "truth" in policy-making is essential.

Politics is a place of many voices and "truths." It is the art of politics to ensure that all voices are heard, appreciated and considered when creating the rules by which we govern ourselves. I, along with my women colleagues, find that we are the listeners—as well as the doers. Having more women in positions of leadership is what our country needs to create better rules.

I came to politics somewhat late in life, but from the very first moment, I jumped in with enthusiasm and dedication. I am proud that a career in government is the path I have chosen to leave my mark on the world.

~ Senator Carol Liu

Senator Carol Liu represents the 21st District in the State of California. She taught public school for fourteen years before becoming a school administrator and Executive Director of the Richmond Federation of Teachers. Carol was first elected to political office as a member of the La Canada Flintridge City Council. She serves on the Executive Board of the Women's Leadership Network. Her first priority has always been to make the California public school system one of the best in the nation.

Linda LoRe

The Spirit Within

When I was a small child … I thought that success spelled happiness.
I was wrong, happiness is like a butterfly which appears and delights
us for one brief moment, but soon flits away

~ Anna Pavlova, Russian ballerina

When I started my career, if someone said to "Stop and smell the roses," I'd smile and say, "I don't have time to stop. I'll carry the roses with me!"

My mother often said that I went from baby to adult in one giant leap. The first-born of my parents' eight children, I was a natural leader and organizer. After they divorced, my father remarried, and eventually I became the oldest of eleven siblings. In the beginning our small house had only one bathroom so I learned how to negotiate at an early age.

I first became a CEO at the age of seven when I started a club and named myself president. My team and I sold peanuts and lemonade and raised money for worthy causes. As I grew up, my various roles and experiences inspired my vision of climbing to the top of the corporate ladder.

At the age of thirty-six I was appointed president of a nationally recognized company. A high-powered CEO running a real business, my career was glamorous and exciting. I wore designer clothing, traveled first-class, stayed at exclusive hotels around the world and dined at the finest restaurants. But I traveled with a brief case filled with responsibility until stressed and exhausted, my body, mind and soul broke down and surrendered.

The Spirit within was saying, "It's time to find your life's purpose. You must understand who you really are inside to bring yourself to the next level." It became clear that I needed to stop and smell the roses in order to take the next step forward.

My sabbatical included a spiritual quest to the jungles of Peru where I journeyed with four shaman and ten strangers through the remote back tributaries of the Amazon River. My "suite" was about the size of a large shower with a mattress pad on the floor. Traveling with only the bare essentials of life, I felt stripped to my essence, meaning there was nowhere I could go to hide from myself.

The highlights of my trip included learning to conquer fear crossing a 200′ ravine on a log and witnessing the miraculous healing of a shaman bringing an unconscious, dying child back to life after a deadly snake bite. Paddling in a canoe, I watched the most spectacular meteor shower of the century while listening to the mystical music of natives singing and chanting in prayer.

The grand finale was a seven-mile uphill hike to the top of a mist-shrouded mountain and gazing down upon the ancient ruins of Peru's Machu Picchu, one of the Seven Wonders of the World. Suddenly out of the corner of my eye I spotted an enormous 12-inch blue butterfly dancing and pirouetting in mid-air. I had never seen such a spectacular butterfly before. Then I noticed the blue butterfly was chasing a bird! I can't explain it, but in that moment I realized this magnificent creature and I were one with life

I paused to consider that perhaps something more than coincidence had brought the butterfly and I together on the mountain. The very idea filled me with an indescribable feeling of joy. "If I could watch a magnificent butterfly chasing a bird above the ruins of Machu Picchu," I thought, "then anything is possible."

Nothing I've ever done has been as poignant and meaningful as my trip to the Amazon. In the jungle I learned to trust that the Spirit would guide me to the next level, and I realized how little it takes to survive. But a butterfly chasing a bird on a mist-shrouded mountain taught me that happiness is an inward journey—the biggest adventure of all.

~ Linda LoRe

Linda LoRe has been a CEO for twenty-one years for high profile companies including Giorgio Beverly Hills and Frederick's of Hollywood. Linda is the recipient of numerous awards including Woman of Accomplishment, Women's Hall of Fame and Woman of the Year. She is a founding board member of the Youth Mentoring Connection for at-risk youth and serves as a Director of the Trusteeship of the International Women's Forum.

www.lindalore.com

Melanie Lundquist

The Thread of Philanthropy

Oh, it's very nurturing, very satisfying to know you've been of service.
That's what it's about. … And I'm empowering someone and helping
them achieve something.

~ Wallis Annenberg

My heroes growing up were people like my European grandparents who came to America in the early 1900s. I never had the opportunity to know them before they died, but I was always captivated by my mother's stories about how they had helped many needy families during the Great Depression because they had the means to do so.

Even though he was deceased when the Watts Riots broke out in 1965, I was proud to hear how local residents surrounded and protected the business my civic-minded grandfather had built. It was the community's way of honoring the many contributions that he and my grandmother had made while they were alive.

My mother also had a great effect on me. When she started college and joined a sorority in 1925, her goal was to raise funds to create a dental clinic for impoverished children. Today, there is a mobile clinic from the University of Southern California that provides dental care to needy students in local schools, a continuation of my mother's work.

I remember my mother signing me up for various door-to-door fundraising activities while she stayed on the sidewalk. A painfully shy child, it was hard to ring the bell and ask for donations, but I felt happy knowing the money collected would help other people. At some point, the idea that it was my personal responsibility to leave the world a better place for having been here crystallized in my mind.

The thread of philanthropy continued to weave its way through my life. Today, giving back to the community is an important part of my husband's and my relationship. Deeply inspired by philanthropist Warren Buffet, we believe in his philosophy that this is society's money, and at some point it should be distributed back to society for the good of society. We feel very fortunate to be the temporary stewards of this money and the philanthropy that it enables us to do.

I want to contribute more to the world than to just simply write a check. As a result, I become very involved with the people and organizations that we support. For example, I have always been passionate about contributing to education and public schools, and one of my greatest joys is taking inner-city high school seniors shopping for supplies for their dorm rooms before they head off to college.

Recently I took a very special young student shopping for her dorm room. Wanting the experience to be meaningful and fun, I invited her mother to join us. Some of the supplies that the student selected were: a wonderful pink paisley comforter and sheets for her bed, a set of purple towels, and decorative items for the walls.

When we got to the cash register, the student's mother thanked me profusely. Then her daughter said, "I really appreciate everything you've done for me today, but I want you to know that growing up poor in America is not the worst thing in the world. It has made me appreciate everything that I have been given, and it has taught me a lot about life."

This eighteen-year-old student got it! She already understood what it takes some people a lifetime to understand, if they ever do: the amount of money you have in the bank does not define who you are and it should never be an indication of self-worth. This young woman reinforced my belief that there is only one race, the human race, and we are all in it together, whether we like it or not.

It doesn't matter if you've got a million dollars or one dollar to give. The act of reaching out and extending kindness to people in need is what real philanthropy is all about. I honestly believe that the joy I experienced in that moment will produce a ripple effect in ways I can't begin to understand.

~ Melanie Lundquist

Melanie Lundquist, a leading philanthropist in Southern California, is known for her generous support of public school education and health care. She is a founding board member of the Partnership for Los Angeles schools, co-chairs the Capital Campaign for the California Science Center Phase 2, and is a member of Women Moving Millions. Mr. and Mrs. Lundquist have established the Cardiovascular Institute at Torrance Memorial Medical Center where she is a passionate advocate for women's heart health.

Caroline MacDougall

A Gift from Mother Earth

People say to me so often, "Jane, how you can be so peaceful when every-where around you people want books signed, people are asking these questions, and yet you seem so peaceful," and I always answer that it is the peace of the forest that I carry inside.

~ Jane Goodall

My career in the herbal beverage industry has given me the opportunity to visit exotic places around the world from arid mountains in Africa to tropical rainforests throughout Central America and other developing countries. But the peak of my travel adventures, one that ultimately changed my life, occurred in Costa Rica's Monteverde Cloud Forest on a vacation with friends.

Monteverde, 4,662 feet above sea level, is a lush mountainous cloud-covered, incredibly diverse ecosystem. As I climbed up the mountain, dusk was about to settle in. Fascinated and wanting to go deeper into the forest, I wandered onto a little trail and ended up at the foot of a magnificent waterfall.

My senses were overwhelmed by color, scent and sound—the water cascading down a rocky cliff, the buzzing of insects, the song of birds, the musty fragrance of verdant foliage and brilliant flowers. Standing there soaking in the rich biodiversity of nature, my eyes filled with tears. The forest was literally pulsating with vibrant life!

Overcome with gratitude for this extraordinary moment, I fell to my knees and from within my heart came this vow: "I am going to dedicate myself to preserving the rainforest, so there will always be opportunities for people to receive the gift of life from Mother Earth that I am receiving now."

I knew that a critical source of income for people in developing countries comes from foraging in the wild for herbs, tree saps, and ornamental plants. If products from the forest weren't developed to give it economic value, it would be cut down as the population expands. People living in its midst would begin to farm crops for their survival. Helping to preserve the rainforest would be the next chapter of my work. Of course, I had no idea how many paths this vow would eventually lead me down.

I started to realize that my skills, sourcing ingredients in developing countries and bringing them back to the States for manufacturing, would help rainforest preservation by creating new trade to develop sustainable income for impoverished people. Working with honey, vanilla, and herbs for teas, I found ingredients that would give standing forests the economic value to help prevent illegal logging that is decimating forests worldwide.

Then, one night I had a dream about creating a new product using rainforest herbs and I ended up starting my own business! But becoming an entrepreneur took me away from the vow I had made in Monteverde. Unable to devote the time to travel and develop rainforest ingredients, my heart ached knowing that I wasn't fulfilling my promise.

Six years later, I was introduced to a nutritious seed that falls from upper canopy trees over 130 feet tall, which make up about 20% of Central America's rainforests. Called "ramon nuts," the Maya ate these seeds mixed with their corn flour or roasted them for a beverage. Upon tasting a brew made from the roasted nuts, I realized that ramon nuts were the Maya's original coffee alternative.

The ramon nut, a nutritious free food that was going to waste on the forest floor, is my best discovery yet. It took another six years to get the government's permission to begin the wild harvest of these nuts in the Maya Biosphere Reserve. Today, ramon nuts are harvested for my herbal beverages in Guatemala and Honduras, creating jobs and economic opportunity for local villages.

I have spent the last twenty years creating products that use rainforest ingredients. It was impossible to predict where my vow would take me or how it would return just when I thought I had lost my ability to help preserve this vital ecosystem. Success can be found by holding onto your vision with persistence and dedication!

~ Caroline MacDougall

Caroline MacDougall is the founder and creator of Teeccino Herbal Coffees, America's #1 coffee alternative brand. She also creates teas for a number of top tea companies including The Republic of Tea, Yogi Tea, and Organic India. She has pioneered a number of herbs and ingredients from other countries by creating products for United States customers. The best known herbs she has introduced to American consumers are rooibos, the red tea from South Africa, tulsi tea from India, and ramon nuts from Central America.

www.teeccino.com

Kathy E. Magliato, MD

A Moment of Opportunity

*The human heart has hidden treasures, In secret kept, in silence sealed;
The thought, the hopes, the dreams, the pleasures, Whose charms were
broken if revealed.*

~ Charlotte Bronte

Women move through life spinning many plates in the air at the same time. It's easy to get caught up in all the background noise until suddenly a moment of opportunity comes along. If we don't recognize that moment for what it is, the opportunity is lost and we miss the chance to do something truly extraordinary with our lives.

During my first year as a general surgery intern, my job was pretty much to stay out of everybody's way and not kill anyone. On one particular morning, I found myself standing at the surgical board that shows all the cases for the day. There I was, minding my own business, when a panicked nurse grabbed me and said, "You are needed in OR 7 stat!"

She threw me into the operating room where I found myself in the middle of what could only be described as a war zone. There was a lot of yelling; people were running around frantically; blood was everywhere; things were falling and crashing to the floor. In the middle of this chaos was a surgeon standing near an operating able with a person lying on it. The patient's chest was wide open, and his blood was literally shooting up into the air.

The surgeon didn't even look at me. He just shouted, "Get some gloves on and get over here now!" I had never scrubbed in on a cardiac surgery case before, but somehow I figured out what to do. I nervously walked to the operating table, the last place on the planet that I wanted to be. Then the surgeon said something that changed my life forever: "Grab the heart and hold it steady so I can get a few stitches in the hole we have here."

I peered into the open chest cavity, and there was the heart sitting in a bath of blood. To me, it looked like a large, deformed matzo ball floating in tomato soup. Reaching inside the patient's chest, I firmly but gently closed my hand around his heart.

There is a myth that women make good surgeons because they have dainty little hands, but this is not true. I have catcher's mitts for hands and can palm a basketball and hold down thirteen keys on a piano. A large-handed intern was exactly what this surgeon needed to save his patient's life. When I wrapped my hand around the heart, I was able to cradle and stabilize it perfectly so the surgeon could stitch the hole shut.

It was amazing—a human heart beating in my hand and trying to get free of my grip. The only way to describe it was that I felt like an astronaut who has the rare privilege of walking on the moon, an unbelievable honor that not many people get to have in a lifetime. Inspired and in awe, I looked at the surgeon and asked, "Do you do this every day?"

Annoyed that I would talk during a critical time in the operation, his eyes locked into mine and he said, "Of course, I do. I'm a heart surgeon!" Then he just went back to saving the patient's life as if I had said nothing. My mind was reeling with the possibility that I too could touch the human heart every day!

That was my moment of opportunity—a moment of clarity that told me in no uncertain terms, that this was what I wanted to do with my life. That one single moment became the seed that fueled my passion to spend the next seventeen years training in some of the most brutal and difficult areas of medicine.

When someone wants to know what motivates me to keep doing what I'm doing, my answer is: time. Time motivates me because time is a gift. You and I are only given a certain amount of heartbeats in our lifetime and we need to use them to the best of our ability because we never know how many we will get.

The idea that life is a sequence of moments is fascinating to me because I don't measure time by minutes, hours or days. I measure time by heartbeats and moments and try to find fulfillment in each and every one of them.

~ Kathy E. Magliato, MD, MBA, FACS

Dr. Kathy Magliato, Director of Women's Cardiac Services at St. John's Medical Center in Santa Monica, is one of the few female cardiothoracic surgeons in the world. She is the author of "Heart Matters: A Memoir of a Female Heart Surgeon." Highlighted by the media as an expert in heart disease, she is a sought-after lecturer around the world. Kathy is the recipient of many honors including the Women's Leadership Exchange Compass Award and the American Red Cross Spirit of Humanitarianism Award.

Note: From *Healing Hearts: A Memoir of a Female Heart Surgeon* by Kathy E. Magliato, MD, © 2010 by Kathy Magliato. Used by permission of Broadway Books, a division of Random House, Inc.

Areva D. Martin, Esq.

Miracle Moment

Where there is great love, there are always miracles.

~ Willa Cather, author

When my beautiful two-year-old son was diagnosed with autism nearly ten years ago, I discovered that as a mother and as a woman, I was much stronger than I ever knew.

I was absolutely devastated when the doctor described a disability that would prevent my son from growing up the same way as other little boys. Immediately, I thought of all the things he wouldn't be able to do with his two older sisters and all the opportunities he would miss in his life. It felt like a terrible thief had robbed my family of our hopes and dreams for this precious child.

The autism came out of nowhere. I knew nothing about this disorder and never suspected that my concerns about my son's developmental growth would lead to this diagnosis. Later as I sat in a rocking chair in my son's room, I was shocked, angry and depressed.

Like anyone who suffers an enormous loss, I had a big decision to make. Do I succumb to the pressure and go into a state of depression? Or do I accept this challenge and help my family through what was going to be a difficult period of grief and pain? Was my son's autism really that much different from any other obstacle that life puts in our path?

It felt as if my world was crumbling, but in that moment a miracle occurred. My inner voice said to tackle this problem with every bit of strength that I had. It whispered, "Confront this. You can handle it. Everything will be okay."

I realized that I had the ability to turn my son's illness into an opportunity and make something good happen for other grieving families. The love I had for this beautiful child could overcome anything. I would use my voice to fight for my son's future and for other children who suffered from this terrible disease!

My son has made much progress and has given me more love than I ever could have imagined. He teaches our entire family lessons about kindness, patience, tolerance and the importance of coming together and rising to the occasion.

The moral of my story is this: listen to your inner voice when life unexpectedly throws you an enormous challenge. You really are much stronger than you know.

~ Areva D. Martin, Esq.

Areva Martin is a nationally recognized expert on autism and co-founder and President of Special Needs Network, a non-profit organization for families with special needs children. Founder and managing partner of Martin & Martin, LLP, she is a distinguished lawyer, public speaker and author of two books: "The Everyday Advocate, How to Stand up for Your Child with Special Needs" and "Journey to the Top."

www.martin-martin.net   *www.specialneedsnetwork.org*

Nancy McFadden

A Life Well-Lived

A life not lived for others, is not a life.

~ Mother Teresa

When my mother passed away in the same hospital where she had worked for nearly forty years, I learned things about her that I never knew.

My father left our family when I was eleven, and my mother raised my brother and me as a single parent. A registered nurse, she worked the nightshift in order to take care of her children during the day. I've always believed that the reason my mother experienced so many health problems in mid-life was because she literally exhausted herself. Sadly, at the young age of sixty-nine, she suffered a serious stroke.

The doctors weren't sure if this was the end, but I remained hopeful that mom would pull through. It was late December 1999, and my mother was determined to see the new century. She made it, but only by a matter of days.

I was at her side the entire time. What I remember most was the constant parade of hospital staff — doctors, nurses, janitors, cleaning women, volunteers and nurses' aides — who stopped by to visit every day and night. Drifting in and out of consciousness, many times my mother didn't even know that other people were in the room.

The stories they shared about her absolutely amazed me! I always knew my mother was a strong woman who devoted herself to her children, and I was aware that she was constantly striving to be a good nurse. But I never understood the powerful impact my mother had on people whom I hadn't met.

Like the young woman who explained that she went back to college because of my mother's encouragement. Another woman, devastated when her husband suddenly ended their marriage, said my mother had given her pep talks that helped her to get on with life. A series of people talked about the compassion, support and humor that my mother had brought to their lives over the years.

I didn't know these things because my mother never talked about them. I was surprised that she had the time, the energy, and the generosity of spirit to affect so many people in such a positive way. These inspiring stories were an affirmation of the real hero that my mother was, and they deepened my love and respect for the person whom I loved and respected more than any other.

Until then I always worried that my mother never had the opportunity to enjoy what I thought should be a full life: she worked too hard; she didn't have many material things, and she never went on any big trips round the world. But she had two children who adored her. She had a meaningful career, and her short life had made a difference to more people than I ever realized while she was still alive.

The stories about my mother made me think about how I interacted one-on-one with the people in my life, those I live with, work with, and the people I might encounter once or twice. It made me realize that everything my mother did, she did with love, humor and empathy. The moment I fully understood this other side of my mother, I came to appreciate that this is what a life well-lived is really all about.

~ Nancy McFadden

Nancy McFadden serves as Executive Secretary for Legislation, Appointments, and Policy for Governor Jerry Brown of California. Before that, she served in significant roles in both public and private sectors, including one as a senior official in the Clinton Administration. She is a member of the San Francisco Fine Arts Museum and formerly served on the Board of Directors for the California Museum of History, Women and the Arts, and the Women's Foundation of California.

Sara Miller McCune

Recognizing a Fortuitous Moment

*The ultimate goal is for students to value discourse as a way of being
in the world and addressing the problems of the day.*

~ Deanna Kuhn, professor of
psychology & educaiton

I started my publishing company in January 1965 with $500 in capital, half of which was the valuation of a used air conditioner in my office. With so little start-up capital, the company needed to bring in positive cash flow from day one, especially since I had already filed papers to become a corporation with only a general idea of what I was going to publish.

After considering several possibilities, the merits of starting with a scholarly journal and publishing a booklist around it quickly took on great appeal. I had many friends in this growing field of academia and knew there weren't a lot of scholarly journals being published in the fledging interdisciplinary fields of the social sciences.

But I didn't know how or where I was going to find a scholarly journal just waiting to be launched.

On the evening of the day that my official incorporation papers arrived, I was having drinks with my former political science professor and mentor who had been lamenting the fact that the City University of New York did not have a university press for a journal that she wanted to start. Maybe it was the scotch (although I prefer to think it was fate and the recognition of an exciting opportunity) but I immediately offered to publish her journal through my new company.

We signed a contract the next day, and the first issue of my former professor's journal was published nine months afterwards. Forty-six years later, this same journal is still on my company's list of over 600 journals distributed throughout five continents. From that tiny seed, the foundation of a large corporation grew and flourished.

Looking back on that fortuitous moment, I realized the value of recognizing opportunity when it knocks on your door. As a result, I lead a company that employs 1100 employees and is still privately owned, profitable and independent.

~ Sara Miller McCune

Sara Miller McCune is the Founder and Executive Chairman of Sage Publications, one of the leading academic publishing houses in the world. She is also President of the McCune Foundation and Executive Chairman of the Miller-McCune Center for Research, Media and Public Policy.

www.sagepub.com

Note: Adapted from BEING SAGE: *Memories of the First 45 Years* by Sara Miller McCune. Copyright © 2010 SAGE Publications, Inc.

Judi Sheppard Missett

Following My Passion

It's what I've always wanted to do — to share the laughing, the fun and the appetite, all of it through dance.

~ Martha Graham, American
dancer & choreographer

About forty years ago a tiny little idea and my passion for dancing turned into an opportunity unlike anything I had ever envisioned for myself. Evolving from jazz teacher and performer to business-woman and CEO of an international fitness company was never on my agenda — and certainly not something that I ever thought I'd want to do.

I fell in love with dancing at a very young age. At the age of eleven, I had my own studio in the basement of my family's home and charged seventy-five cents to teach children in my neighbor-hood how to dance. By the age of fourteen, I was a professional per-former and continued to work professionally while I earned my degree from Northwestern University in theatre, radio, and television.

The light bulb went on when I was a dance instructor in Chicago. Lots of women would come to one class, but then they wouldn't come back. It bothered me because I wanted them to really feel the joy of movement and understand what dancing could do for their bodies. When I asked a few students why people weren't returning to my classes, they said that many women didn't really want to be a professional dancer; they just wanted to look like one.

At that moment I thought, well, okay, it's time to make some changes. I started by taking the mirrors down and ramping the music up. Based on my jazz techniques, I made the next set of classes fun and easy to follow. Not only did the health and fitness levels of my students improve, but the classes became so popular that I had to turn people away!

I always thought my career path was to be in theater, but the direction of my life changed completely when I discovered my love of dance could help women feel and look better as well as lift their spirits and improve their self-esteem. They were not only happier within themselves, but they were better for their families, co-workers and friends. As my role as an entrepreneur evolved and Jazzercise continued to grow, I empowered thousands of other women to become successful in business as instructors and franchisors owners.

If there is one lesson I can share, it is this—if you follow your passion, you will never fail. Be willing to embrace change and reinvent yourself when the opportunity arises. I love what I do and do what I love as a teacher, a performer, and a CEO. And it all began when my mind was opened to new and exciting possibilities just because of a little idea.

~ Judi Sheppard Missett

Judi Sheppard Missett, *fitness advocate and aerobic fitness pioneer, founded Jazzercise, Inc. in 1969. Today, the international dance fitness company has 7,800 instructor franchisees in all 50 states and 32 countries. Judi has received many honors that include dozens of leadership and lifetime achievement awards such as induction into the Enterprising Women Hall of Fame, the International Association of Fitness Professionals Hall of Fame and the President's Award from the Women Presidents' Organization.*

www.jazzercise.com

Holly J. Mitchell

A Collective Responsibility

... if any community is going to be seen at its best ... the women in that community have to be viewed as equally important as the men. And women have to be able to live outside of boundaries that are placed on them because of their gender. As well as their race or religion.

~ Anita Hill

When I was a fifteen-year-old African-American teenager in the 1980s, I believed that I was a direct beneficiary of our mothers' and grandmothers' hard-won political and social accomplishments. I found comfort in the convenient assumption that the rights I enjoyed would be the rights that I would always have—until the day the Ku Klux Klan appeared on my high school campus in Riverside County.

Coming out of math class with a group of white friends, I was horrified when our school was suddenly invaded by hundreds of clansman dressed in full KKK regalia: white robes, masks and hoods. On motorcycles and bicycles they were terrorizing students and distributing hate-filled literature against people of color.

I couldn't believe what was happening! Panicked students were running and screaming in different directions. Knowing that my safety was at risk, a surge of adrenaline rushed through my body. I have to get out of here! Where should I go? What should I do? No disaster drill I ever had prepared me for something like this.

A second-generation native Californian, I was instantly propelled into a space that I did not believe still existed in America. It was shocking to think there were people who wanted my rights to be taken away because I was black! It was a rude awakening, and in that moment I took off my rose-colored glasses and began to grow up.

In the weeks and months that followed, I watched my mother step up to the plate on behalf of minority students who faced suspension or expulsion because of their violent reaction in the midst of utter chaos. She made me realize that the leadership of women was essential if my school and community were to survive this devastating experience.

That was when I started to find my own social consciousness. At fifteen that meant understanding how people in the outside world, excluding my classmates, friends, and neighbors, viewed me as an African-American female. It was about recognizing who I am as a person, embracing my differences and learning to feel comfortable in my own skin. In the process it became crystal clear that I could no longer afford to be complacent about critical issues of inequality and social injustice.

I believe it is essential for women of all ages to make use of their natural leadership ability. This doesn't necessarily mean running for office; it means tapping into your heart to identify and take action on those issues that resonate with you—perhaps childcare, health care, elder care, education, poverty, domestic violence or city planning.

We share a collective responsibility to protect the comforts that we and our families are privileged to enjoy in America. They have been hard fought by others and should never be taken for granted.

~ Assemblymember Holly J. Mitchell

Holly J. Mitchell (D-Los Angeles) serves the 47th Assembly District of California. She comes to the Assembly from leadership in the nonprofit sector where, as CEO of Crystal Stairs, a child development agency, she championed family-focused policymaking. Her commitment to community service and social justice began in elementary school as a student volunteer which eventually led to an extensive record of student activism and a Coro Fellowship in Public Affairs following her undergraduate studies at UC Riverside.

www.hollyjmitchell.com

Rita Moya

The Treasure Room

If we are to achieve a richer culture, rich in contrasting values, we must recognize the whole gamut of human potentialities, and so weave a less arbitrary social fabric, one in which each diverse human gift will find a fitting place.

~ Margaret Mead

I grew up on a farm in a rural area of the Midwest. My mother, one of thirteen children, was a product of that environment too. Her family was very poor and she worked her way through high school and college to become a teacher. Although she didn't have an opportunity to travel, my mother was incredibly worldly with a genuine openness for other cultures, opinions and lifestyles in a way that was quite unusual for her time.

It's difficult to know how my mother developed her extraordinary world view, but it's not hard to understand how I developed mine. In one of the bedrooms of our old farm house, my mother carefully stored and stacked every issue of Life Magazine according to year from the 1940's on. As a child I loved to go with my mother into what we called the "Treasure Room." We would read stories about kings and queens and look at all the pictures of different people in faraway lands.

My friends thought the Treasure Room was the most boring place on earth. They had no interest in looking at my mother's old magazines, but to me, they were the most priceless things my family owned. Even the local library didn't have anything nearly as special.

When I was a teenager, my mother became gravely ill, and I sadly realized that she would never be able to visit any of the amazing places we had read about. Shortly after she lost her battle with cancer at the age of fifty-three, I was given an opportunity to attend college in Vienna, Austria. This first taste of adventure was a chance to fulfill my mother's dreams and inspired me to want to see the rest of the world.

I quickly discovered that my family's farm was just a miniscule piece of an enormous planet. But more importantly, I realized that seeing the world isn't just about visiting other countries—it is an opportunity to grow by experiencing many different ways of thinking and living. There is so much joy to be had by focusing on the commonalities that all people share instead our differences.

Looking back, those precious moments of time spent with my mother in the Treasure Room shaped my life. Learning to appreciate the beauty of the world and all its wondrous cultural diversity was the greatest gift she could have given me.

~ Rita Moya

Rita Moya is the Principal Advisor to The M Fund, a private social enterprise fund and Technology Strategy Advisor to BioIQ, a wellness technology company. She also served as vice president of State Solutions for the United Health Group/Ingenix and chief executive officer of two health foundations: the Foundation for a Healthy Kentucky and the National Health Foundation (NHF). Rita serves on several boards including Direct Relief International, Norton Healthcare Networks and Harvard Kennedy School of Government Leadership Board.

Mary Murphy

Living a Big Life

I don't want to get to the end of my life and find that I have lived just the length of it. I want to have lived the width of it as well.

~ Diane Ackerman

I grew up in St. Louis, Missouri in a very large and very loving close-knit Irish Catholic family. My mother was one of fifteen children; my father was one of eleven. My grandparents, aunts, uncles and cousins all lived in the same neighborhood. Everyone I knew was born in St. Louis and stayed in St. Louis.

Making the decision to attend a private women's Catholic college outside New York City was a big step for a small town girl like me — the first girl in the family to go to college and live away from home. My father worked for the railroad, so it was a given that I would travel to New York by train.

The entire family, about 150 people, showed up at the station to say good-bye. I had been looking forward to that day for months, but ten minutes after the train pulled away, I was overcome with a deep sense of loneliness. I had no idea how much my life was about to change—until the train pulled into Grand Central Station.

I walked off the train and into a whole new world: a bustling, thriving, sophisticated metropolis unlike anything I had ever seen before. At that moment something inside me said, "You are going to live a big life." A young girl about to start college, I didn't understand what the expression "living a big life" meant.

When I got off the next train in Tarrytown, New York, the first thing I saw was a glimmering gold dome sitting on top of a beautiful building that overlooked the Hudson River. I was filled with excitement as my taxi cab headed for the building with the gold dome—my home away from home for the next four years.

I learned more than math, history and political science from the religious community who taught us; I learned about second chances. In my immaturity, I went a little wild, and yet the college saw something in me that I hadn't seen myself—they saw someone worth holding on to, and they viewed my mistakes as things to be learned from, not branded by.

Several years later, an adult and mother of two, I became a writer for TV Guide until my position disappeared as the company began to downsize. Even though my twenty-year career was officially over, I decided to give 100 % to my remaining days. I showed up on time every morning for two months and worked eight to nine hours trusting that if I walked out of the company with dignity, I would walk into my next job with dignity.

That is exactly what happened. I didn't let fear or depression set in. I believed friends, the positive ones, who said the best was yet to come. And it did. A former colleague asked if I would go to Rwanda to cover a story, an amazing opportunity that led to two years of traveling to India, Sri Lanka, and Cambodia, and many other countries around the world. I became a foreign correspondent of sorts, writing not about wars, but about people doing good works.

As I traversed the world, it suddenly dawned on me that I was a risk-taker. I had never perceived myself as one, but it turns out that ever since I got on that train in St. Louis so long ago, I have been taking risks and living a big life after all. And it just keeps getting bigger. A year ago I was hired as on-air correspondent and producer for a nightly television show on a major network!

I view all the different pieces of life as part of the whole. One opportunity leads to another opportunity; different careers weave their way into new careers; successful relationships build upon each other. But something has to start it all in motion—and that is the courage to say yes when the right moment comes to you.

~ Mary Murphy

Mary Murphy, a senior lecturer at the Annenberg School of Communications & Journalism at the University of Southern California, is a senior correspondent for Entertainment Tonight/The Insider, a contributing editor for the Los Angeles Times Magazine, USA Weekend Magazine, The New York Post, The Hollywood Reporter, and The TV Guide Network. Previously, she was the senior writer for TV Guide. She is a loyal supporter of the Los Angeles Midnight Mission on Skid Row where a library is named in her honor.

Debra Nakatomi

The Meaning of Grace

I do not at all understand the mystery of grace — only that it meets us where we are but does not leave us where it found us.

~ Anne La Mott, author

Several years ago I was a fellow of the Asian Pacific American Women's Leadership Institute with nine other women from around the country. Participants were selected on the basis of professional accomplishment, community involvement, and their experience benefitting others, especially girls and young women.

The program included one-on-one sessions with a professional coach to help each woman gain a better understanding of herself as a person inside and out. After spending time together, coaches had to choose one word that they thought described their participant and then share that word with the whole group.

Luminous! Dynamic! Inspiring! These are some examples of the wonderful words that the other coaches used to describe the women in my class. Naturally, I was very curious to hear what word my coach had chosen for me. When she said "Grace," I thought, "Grace? Really? Couldn't she have thought of something else?" Confused and disappointed, I didn't know what to say or what to think.

My initial reaction was that my coach had selected a superficial word based on a quick impression and didn't really know the person I was inside. But as we talked, I became aware that I lacked an understanding of the meaning of "grace" and was unable to fully appreciate the compliment I had been given.

My coach said that to her "grace" meant elegance, dignity, generosity, and kindness. It was about taking care of other people and putting their needs first. "A person with grace," she explained, "strives to live a life of meaning, has the courage to overcome difficulties, and works hard to be a good person." "But that woman is not me," I said with tears in my eyes. "The woman you are describing is my mother!"

A second generation Japanese American, my mother grew up with very little. Her senior year of high school, dreams of college and career as a pediatrician were interrupted by war. Like many other Japanese Americans, she lived for years in a concentration camp; for her it was Gila River in the Arizona desert.

Still, my mother worked hard to overcome her hardships by finding hope in the face of hopelessness and always living with honor and integrity. Grace, the word that I had rejected from my coach, was a gift to me from my mother.

Realizing that I had taken on some of my mother's characteristics was a huge moment of self-awareness. More than ever, I felt happy and proud to be her daughter. I experienced a connectedness with my mother's past and with my present and future in a brand-new way, as if seeing life through a different kind of lens. Because of my mother's influence, I too had grown up striving to live a life of meaning and gratitude.

Through her many acts of love and kindness, my mother proved that joy is always possible even in harsh circumstances. I was touched to realize that in a very short time, my coach was able to recognize some of my mother's grace in me. She is now eighty-seven years old, and I'm often reminded in unexpected ways of the huge imprint this remarkable woman has made upon my life.

~ Debra Nakatomi

__Debra Nakatomi__ is president of Nakatomi & Associates, a strategic communications firm that designs social marketing and media advocacy campaigns promoting access, equity and learning. Debra is International Commissioner and board member of Girl Scouts of the USA. She serves on the board for the Asian Pacific Islander American Health Forum and the Little Tokyo Service Center Community Development Corporation and is a former board chair of the Los Angeles Women's Foundation.

www.nakatomipr.com

Anna Ouroumian

Daring to Dream

What you Dare to Dream, Dare to Do

~ Anonymous

I was only a few months old when I was put in an orphanage in Beirut, Lebanon, the first of ten that I would live in until I was a teenager. Less than a year later, my newborn sister joined me in the same orphanage. My very ill mother was unable to take care of her children, and my father, an alcoholic, had abandoned us. Later he died in the civil war that was raging throughout Lebanon.

Eventually, my sister and I were sent to an all-girls Catholic orphanage and school on the demarcation line separating East and West Beirut, the Christian and Muslim sides respectively. Destruction was everywhere. Sandbags surrounded the school; we could see bullet holes and big gaping crates on the walls of neighboring buildings. As part of the multi-national forces, French parachutists were posted across the street from our school, only a few feet away.

My dream was to go to college, but all I ever heard was that I needed to get a job as soon as possible. I excelled in my classes and skipped several grades, but the nuns wanted me to be in the technical track to ensure that I could get a secretarial job after ninth grade. Begging, pleading and arguing about how much I loved learning, I persuaded the principal to let me pursue the regular track, my path to more education. But the orphanage didn't have a high school, and I had to find a way to attend on my own.

I was determined to make my dream come true! So once again I plotted and planned, argued and cajoled, to put into place the two things that could make it possible for me to continue my education: a place to stay—and a way to pay for high school.

I knew that what I was asking had never been done before in this very conservative, hierarchical, religious environment. The country was in chaos. The war was still raging. It was a big risk for a young girl like me because the nuns could have decided that I was just a trouble-maker and not even let me finish there. But looking back, they must have seen something special in me.

When they agreed that I could board at the orphanage and attend high school across town, I was ecstatic. At my request, one of the nuns even convinced a priest to find a benefactor to help pay for my high school. My plan worked. My prayers were answered!

The war was raging stronger than ever when the long awaited school year began in September, but it did not matter that I had to walk thirty minutes each way with bombs going off all around me. It did not matter that I had to sleep on a sponge cot on the floor of a theater turned into a makeshift shelter with two hundred other girls. It did not matter that I had to study in a smelly single stall bathroom with running water on the floor and wind seeping in from the top and bottom of a poorly fitted door.

What mattered was that I was given a chance to attend high school. It was a long-shot dream for a little girl with the odds stacked against her, and I welcomed the sacrifices.

One day on my way back from school, I noticed a building across the street that seemed strangely familiar. My heart started to beat furiously! Was this my first orphanage? Overcome with emotion and memories of a scared toddler crying in her crib and waiting for her mother to come and take her home, I tiptoed over to the playground. Yes! This was my first orphanage!

Wiping away tears, I realized that my life had come full-circle — and a long way from this sad place. According to statistics for girls of my social class, I was only destined for a second grade education, but I had beaten the odds. Now I could hope to go to college!

That moment I realized a very valuable life lesson: to always take big "calculated" risks and to not be afraid to ask. These experiences paved the way for my incredible and miraculous subsequent journey to America, the land of all possibilities. It also paved the way for my work with thousands of primarily underserved inner-city youth teaching them to go after their wildest dreams too.

~ Anna Ouroumian

Anna Ouroumian attended UCLA. Having received the Outstanding Senior Award as one of four out of 10,500 seniors, she was the only student highlighted at graduation. She is the Refounder & CEO of the Academy of Business Leadership, and the youngest member of the Women's Leadership Board at Harvard and the Trusteeship. A past founding board member of the Women's Foundation of California, she was featured in Forbes and other outlets, and is the recipient of honors such as the Inspiration Award from National Association of Women Business Owners.

www.goabl.org

Eileen E. Padberg

Standing on Common Ground

As a woman, I have no country. As a woman the world is my country.

~ Virginia Woolf, English author

My entire career has been focused on politics and policy issues affecting all women and their constitutional rights. So when I was asked to prepare a plan that would enable Iraqi women to share in the financial rewards of an emerging democracy by helping them to get the training needed to become entrepreneurs or advance in their government jobs, I was very excited.

Believing that women everywhere need the same things—opportunities and a level playing field, I thought that if Iraqi women had a stake in their economy by creating and building new businesses, democracy would have a better chance to succeed. But when I tried to put on a gas mask for the first time, the real risks of going to Iraq sank in.

After being shown how to use the gas mask in the event of a biological weapons attack, I was handed a helmet and a thirty-pound flak jacket that left me feeling crushed by the weight. What it would be like to wear this outfit in the scorching heat of the Iraqi desert?

In a few days I was scheduled to board a U.S. Air Force Cargo plane to Iraq where I would be transferred to an armored bus and taken to the Green Zone, a heavily guarded, five square mile compound. For the next six months my new "home" would be surrounded by concrete barriers and barbed wire.

Although I had been in tough situations to promote democracy and women's rights in third world countries before, this was the first time there was a price tag on my life. Anyone who kidnapped or killed an American woman would receive a $300,000 reward. Bombs and mortar attacks sometimes missed my trailer by only a few feet. Clearly, this was the ultimate test of my commitment to improve women's lives.

When I met the women business leaders of Iraq, they were well-educated and well-dressed. Each one had suffered many tragedies of war especially the loss of husbands, fathers and sons who were kidnapped, tortured or killed. Traditionally, it was a man's responsibility to support the family, but now Iraqi women knew it was up to them.

My six-month assignment grew into twenty-two months. Not one moment went by when I wasn't inspired by their tenacity and unshakeable faith in the future. I fell in love with their contagious laughter and marveled at how they would tease and joke with me. It was sometimes said that they had to laugh or they would never stop crying. My thirty-pound flak jacket was lightweight compared to the burdens these women carried.

I saw heroism in these courageous women who traveled miles of treacherous desert roads dodging bullets, gunfire and blinding sandstorms. Enduring suffocating heat and long hours of standing in lines at security checkpoints, they never knew for sure if they would arrive home safely. They risked their lives learning the skills necessary to help start new businesses and rebuild their country.

Women everywhere stand on common ground with dignity, determination, compassion, and commitment, drawing upon whatever strength is necessary to better our world.

~ Eileen E. Padberg

Eileen E. Padberg, president of Eileen Padberg Consulting, is active in organizations for women including Women in Leadership, The International Women's Forum/The Trusteeship, and Republican Majority for Choice and WisePlace. Honors include YWCA Woman of the Year, Woman Sage, Excellence in Leadership, and the National Association of Women Business Owners Remarkable Woman Award.

www.eileenpadberg.com

Judy Patrick

Working with Heart

No matter what we do, we can make it our ministry. No matter what form our job or activity takes, the content is the same as everyone else's; we are here to minister to human hearts.

~ Marianne Williamson

I had been enjoying my job at a major communications company and was being promoted fairly quickly. Then I started to wonder why I was doing work that, for me, didn't have heart.

Sometime later I casually mentioned to my father that I hadn't gone to work one day that week because I had been sick, and he said, "I never missed a day of work in my life." My first thought was "Big deal. This isn't necessarily a value that I hold."

Then he went on to say, "There has never been a day in my life when I didn't want to go to work." That caught my attention. I immediately knew that having a job I was eager to go to every day was something I really wanted.

This was the start of a four-year journey for work that had heart. Of course, I had to discover what kind of work had heart. But first I needed to figure out how to cut the golden handcuffs of a lucrative salary, good benefits, and retirement and stock options.

Fortunately, my company was in the midst of a big divesture process and needed to reduce their workforce. Accepting the offer of a one year leave of absence with ongoing benefits, I decided to take the year off, rent my house, and travel.

My partner and I devised an elaborate itinerary of adventure, but we only did one thing on the itinerary, a canoe trip through the Oikekenoki Swamp. It became clear that the next part of the year needed to be about quiet reflection and making time to just sit still.

I thought my quest for stillness would be the beginning of an internal journey about my next work. Instead, what began to come into my consciousness was the sexual abuse I had experienced as a child from a neighbor and an older cousin. Somehow, I managed to repress these traumatic incidents by always working hard and striving for excellence.

Having grown up in a family where it was believed that a hard day's work could cure anything, I realized that I needed to face my past and heal the wounds of abuse before making the transition to finding a job with heart. The better part of the year was spent coming to terms with my feelings about what had happened and doing physically demanding work that required little intellect such as orchard work and house painting.

Looking back, it was a good thing that I couldn't see around the first bend in the road because I might not have had the courage to go forward. It ultimately proved to be a very emotional journey of self-discovery that transformed my life, but the stops along the way were not always pleasurable. When the year was up, I was finally able to return to the original question: "What work would have heart for me?

After much contemplation, I decided that I really wanted the next step of my career to be in a nonprofit organization that focused on women and girls living in poverty. At first I struggled with the belief that it wouldn't even be possible to find a job in the nonprofit sector that could pay me enough money to live on.

I developed a mantra and repeated it over and over saying "I am now doing work that I really believe in and am making enough money to meet my basic needs." About a month later I saw an ad for a position in a local nonprofit organization—working with low-income women and girls! My education and experience fit perfectly with what they were looking for. I was offered the job, and it became the entry into my life work.

Thirty years later, I am still living the vision seized upon in a casual moment of conversation with my father—having a job that I want to do to each and every day. My twelve-year career with the Women's Foundation of California is definitely a job with heart. What could be better than having the opportunity to work with dedicated people in an organization that has transformed the lives of countless people and strives to create a more just and equitable world for women and girls?

Hopefully, I have inspired you to set out on your own journey of self-discovery, even if you can't yet see the end of road. This may very well be the road that leads to your transformation. But whatever path you ultimately choose, find work that has meaning and speaks to your heart.

~ Judy Patrick

Judy Patrick is the President and Chief Executive Officer of the Women's Foundation of California. Prior to her appointment in 2008, she held the post of Executive Vice President of Programs for nine years. In that role Judy led the Foundation's advocacy and policy change work including the development of the groundbreaking Women's Policy Institute. A former researcher and program evaluator in both the public and private sectors, she serves on numerous boards of directors.

www.womensfoundca.org

Kavita N. Ramdas

A Farmer's Words

When I dare to be powerful – to use my strength in the service of my vision, then it becomes less and less important whether I am afraid.

~ Audre Lourdes, Caribbean-American writer

I was privileged to be born into a middle class family in Delhi, India where I had many opportunities and received a good education. But I dropped out of college after failing my exams in my second year, not sure of what I wanted to do or be.

My mother, who had always been active in social justice, immediately found me volunteer work at a rural community-based organization, saying simply, "it will be good for you to see how most of India has to live." This took me to one of the most impoverished villages in the country. I felt very connected to the people in this small farming community and was convinced that I had found my life's work.

One day I wanted to help local farm women separate wheat from the chaff. I watched carefully as they held a basket in both hands and skillfully tossed the wheat into the air over and over again. The chaff, which is very light, separates and flies away. The heavier wheat then falls into the basket. But when I tried, I dropped all the wheat because I had no idea what I was doing.

I didn't know anyone was watching until an old farmer asked me to come over and talk to him. "You know, daughter," he said. "I don't think you are ever going to be a good farmer. You are dropping more wheat on the ground than you are getting into the basket.

"You are able to read and write. Anyone in our village would give an arm and a leg to have the education that you have. So many girls can't even go to school, and here you are. Tell me why you are here."

"Well, I've come to help you," I said with great sincerity. "I want to make your life easier. I feel very bad that you have to live in such poverty." And then this elderly, uneducated farmer spoke the words that changed my life.

He said, "If you really feel that bad, then why don't you use the skills that you do have. You have been blessed with the privilege of an education. Why don't you go home and tell the rest of the world how we live and what is happening here? Why don't you use your skills more efficiently than trying to help us farm?"

At the age of nineteen, this was a big lesson for me. I realized the true value of an education and knew I needed to finish college so I could be a better advocate for justice and equality — the things I really cared about. In just one quiet, reflective moment, a farmer's words shifted my whole idea of how I was going to live the rest of my life.

It is important to appreciate the gifts we are given. Women must take full advantage of their skills and strengths to confidently pursue the things we value and need to fight for. There are many different ways to serve the world, and the world needs the very best that we can give.

~ Kavita N. Ramdas

Kavita N. Ramdas *is the Executive Director of Ripples to Waves, a program on Social Entrepreneurship and Development at Stanford University. She is the former President and CEO of the Global Fund for Women, an international grant making foundation that advances women's human rights worldwide. The recipient of numerous philanthropic and leadership awards, Kavita chairs the Women in Public Service Initiative of the U.S. State Department led by Secretary of State Hillary Clinton.*

fsi.stanford.edu   *www.globalfundforwomen.org*

Marguerite Rangel

Taking the Plunge

The water doesn't know what age you are when you jump in, so why not?

~ Dara Torres, Olympic swimmer

I grew up in a small town on the San Francisco Bay with its public pool situated on a hill. Even in the summer, cold morning winds blow onto the hill from the bay but disappear in the midday heat. It was at this pool that I learned to swim.

Public swimming lessons for children took place on early, brisk summer weekday mornings. We learned the basics in the large pool with daily lessons culminating in the diving pool as mothers watched their children's progress from bleachers nearby.

I still remember the first time I jumped off a diving board at the age of six. The water in the fifteen-foot pool looked impossibly deep, and when I took my place on the board, I could not move! At first I could hear my classmates yelling for me to jump. I don't know how long I stood motionless on the board, but I slowly became aware that silence had befallen the scene. The usually chatting mothers became mute, and as my shivering wet classmates joined them, all eyes were on me. The only sound was my coach's voice, patiently, steadily encouraging me to jump.

In one sudden burst of faith, I plunged into the pool and swam quickly to the surface. The freedom that I felt from overcoming my fear was complete and total exhilaration! That memory has never left me. It has served as a metaphor for my life and has given me courage during those times when I needed it most.

One of those times was deciding to live in Paris during the year between college and law school. In my traditional Mexican-American family, daughters are expected to always stay close to home. But I dreamt of the Parisian life, so when I graduated from college, I bought a one-way ticket and arrived in the City of Lights with one hundred dollars.

I stuffed my suitcase into a locker and went to an agency in search of a job. At the end of the day, I retrieved my suitcase, got on a subway train and thought, "I don't know anyone in this city. If something were to happen to me, no one would know. What am I doing here all alone?"

I turned to look at the Eiffel Tower glowing against a backdrop of a breathtaking pink sunset. At that very moment it felt as if God had tapped me on the shoulder and said, "Don't be afraid. Get ready to start an exciting adventure. Enjoy it to the fullest! This is why you are here!" With that, I jumped into French life and experienced one of the most magnificent years I've ever had.

After returning to the United States for law school, I married, had two children and worked as an attorney. Years later I didn't want to practice law. Afraid of growing old and looking back with regret about chances I hadn't taken, at forty-four I decided to try something different. I had no idea what challenges lay ahead or if I could even be successful. But I leapt into it just as I had jumped into the pool of my childhood and was blessed to find a most deeply satisfying and fulfilling new career.

I love to dream big dreams. That has never changed. I am more determined than ever to let my imagination run wild and take big, delicious bites out of everything the world has to offer. If I start to feel nervous about trying something new, I picture a frightened little girl standing on diving board and remember how exhilarating it can be to take a risk.

Life is meant to be an exciting adventure! Jump in!

~ Marguerite Rangel

Marguerite Rangel, JD CLU ChFC is a principal of RSG Financial of Pacific Advisors, Inc., a California-based financial services firm focusing on all aspects of financial planning for individuals and businesses with special knowledge in charitable and investment planning, estate tax issues, executive benefits and business succession. A longtime member of the State Bar of California, she is a member of the National Association of Women Business Owners and serves as a trustee of the Los Angeles chapter's foundation.

Connie Rice

Claiming My Destiny

Every woman needs to have a feeling of control over her own destiny.

~ Maya Angelou

I have known women like my grandmother and aunt, who before they died, told me with tears in their eyes that I had given them so much happiness because I did what they had never been able to do. They loved watching me live life on my terms and regretted never having the opportunity to claim their destiny. These older women said they enjoyed living vicariously through the accomplishments of younger women like me.

I was in the eleventh grade when I heard African-American congresswoman, Barbara Jordan's impassioned speech during the Nixon impeachment hearings prompted by the Watergate scandal in 1974. Absolutely mesmerized by this courageous woman's power to marshal the history of the country and command the attention of the congressional room, I listened in awe:

Earlier today, we heard the Preamble to the Constitution of the United States. "We, the people." It is a very eloquent beginning. But when that document was created on the 17th of September 1787, I was not included … I felt … left out by mistake. But through the power of amendment, interpretation, and court decisions, I have been included in, "We, the people." … I am not going to sit here and be an idle spectator to the diminution, the subversion, the destruction of the Constitution.

By the time the hearings were over, I was transformed into a budding civil rights activist. I had claimed my destiny! It didn't matter that no one else in my family had ever gone to law school before. At the age of seventeen, I knew what I wanted to do with my life — become one of the top civil rights attorney's in the country and fight for underserved, poor, and minority populations.

When I started law school on a scholarship, it was required that I work thirty hours a week. Swept up in working on projects in poverty law and civil rights around the country, I actually worked sixty to eighty hours a week. As a result, I wasn't aware of all the ins and outs of graduating law school, and I underestimated the importance of getting a clerkship after I finished.

I also didn't understand that getting a clerkship is an extremely competitive process. But I did learn that that I would need an outstanding recommendation from a professor. So I chose one whom I thought knew me well and had seen first-hand how hard I worked and how well I performed under pressure.

A great debater and fascinated by trials, I always dreamed of becoming a litigator. I felt confident that I could be very persuasive in front of a jury. When I asked my professor for a letter of recommendation, he said, "Of course, I will write you a letter. But it will only be for the District Court. You're good, but not good enough for the Court of Appeals." I just looked at him and said, "Why did you have to tell me that? Now I can only apply to the Court of Appeals!"

I always thought my destiny was to be a litigator for the District Court, but in one moment everything changed. Because my professor said that I wasn't qualified for the Court of Appeals, I had to prove that I was qualified. It became absolutely imperative to stand up for my own ability and show that he was wrong.

My first interview with a Court of Appeals circuit judge was with an amazing man who was truly a legend in his time. We talked about everything, but what I appreciated most was his sharp intellect and feeling that he was comfortable dealing with smart, independent women. After an hour, I knew that we were meant to work together. So I said, "You need to hire me now. You know that I am the right clerk for you." He looked at me in total surprise! But I got the job.

In retrospect, my pride in having to show my professor that he was wrong paid off by forcing me to raise the bar. Landing that clerkship, I earned a credential that catapulted me to the top of my profession. I also learned that as you rise in power, you don't have to lose empathy or compassion. Real leaders become even more understanding and caring about the people they are privileged to serve.

My clerkship lasted for two years. It was an honor when the judge asked me to stay on for life, a rare opportunity in law. But if I wanted to become one of the top civil rights attorneys in the country, I couldn't play it safe. I needed to take a risk, move on and get out in the world. "Thank you for everything," I said to my brilliant mentor, "but I can't accept your offer. I have a destiny to claim."

I have never forgotten the many brave women who paved the way for my success. They were the ones who opened the doors for me to walk through. I have chosen a life of risk, but today, thanks to their courage, that is okay. I am fortunate to have been born in this country during a time when women have the opportunity to soar.

Love yourself enough to find your passion. Claim your destiny, whatever it might be, and do what truly matters to you.

~ Connie Rice

Connie Rice is a prominent civil rights activist and attorney and co-founder/co-director of the Advancement Project in Los Angeles. She has received over 50 major awards for her work in expanding opportunity and advancing multi-racial democracy. Connie has been named one of California's Top 10 most influential lawyers. She is the author of "POWER CONCEDES NOTHING: One Woman's Quest for Social Justice in America, from the Courtroom to the Kill Zones."

www.advancementprojectca.org

Susan J. Rose

A Passion for Politics

In politics if you want anything said, ask a man. If you want anything done, ask a woman.

~ Margaret Thatcher

When I was a freshman in college, I became interested in government and enjoyed politics so much that an instructor invited me to take an upper division class during my second year. Fascinated with the political process, I asked my professor what courses I needed to take to prepare for a career in government. "That's not possible," he said. "You're a woman. The only thing you'll ever be able to do is teach."

I didn't understand the full impact his remark had on me until years later when I thought about how my professor had narrowed my perspective on what I could accomplish with my life. Like many young women at the time, after graduation I married my college sweetheart and gave birth to two children in my early twenties.

For the next several years, I trekked around the country supporting my husband's career, teaching school, taking care of our daughters and trying to be the perfect wife. Eventually, I began to wonder how I had arrived at this place in life—living in a city that I didn't like and becoming a mother at such an early age. I couldn't understand why the decisions I had made left me feeling lonely and unfulfilled.

Author Betty Friedan's groundbreaking book, *The Feminine Mystique*, published in 1963 put the pieces of the puzzle together:

> *The problem lay buried, unspoken for many years in the minds of American women. It was a strange stirring, a sense of dissatisfaction, a yearning that women suffered in the middle of the twentieth century in the United States. Each suburban housewife struggled with it alone ...she was afraid to ask even of herself the silent question – "Is this all?"*

The experts said that all we had to do to be truly satisfied was to surrender our dreams.

> *Truly feminine women do not want a career, higher education or political rights. They bake their own bread, sew their own clothes and keep their "new washing machines and dryers running all day" pitying the unhappy women who want to be poets, physicists or presidents.*

Surrendering my dreams was the path that I had taken. This realization helped me to better understand myself and the different choices I had made.

We moved to California when my daughters were in preschool. I remember looking at pictures in their reading text books and feeling as if my own life was being repeated. The pictures showed a little boy working in the garage with his father and his tools and a little girl wearing an apron preparing dinner with her mother in the kitchen.

Knowing the same "problem" would happen to my daughters and other young girls, I became involved in a national effort to analyze and evaluate text books that stereotyped gender roles. My first successful foray into government was lobbying the California Board of Education to adopt nonsexist policies for educational reading materials. My fascination for politics was re-ignited! I went back to college and received a second Master's Degree in Public Administration.

These key moments led me to a career in local government. My professor steered me down a path that didn't fit with who I was, and Betty Friedan opened my eyes to the power of making my own creative choices. Finally, my experience with my daughters' elementary school books instilled an undying passion for women's issues, and I realized that politics was the best way for me to create change and make a difference.

I have worked for city, county and state governments and eventually won an elected position to my local Board of Supervisors for two terms. Today my time is focused on recruiting and mentoring younger women to run for public office because these women will make the changes that affect our lives and the lives of girls who follow in their footsteps. The battle for women's equality has come a long way, but it's not over yet!

"The problem that has no name," Betty Friedan wrote decades ago, "may well be the key to our future as a nation and a culture. We can no longer ignore that voice within women that says: *I want something more than my husband, my children and my home.*"

For me that "something" has meant achieving personal fulfillment through a rewarding career in local government and encouraging all women to follow their dreams.

~ Susan J. Rose

Susan J. Rose, *honored by the California State Legislature for her efforts on behalf of women and girls, was recognized as Santa Barbara's Democratic Woman of the Year and was inducted into the California Women Leaders Hall of Fame. A founding member of the county's Women's Political Committee, she served as the Executive Director of the Los Angeles City Commission on the Status of Women. Currently, Susan is working with Antioch University Santa Barbara to create a women in leadership program.*

Cheryl Saban, Ph.D.

A Shift in Perspective

Your thoughts don't always give you an accurate picture of reality, yet your mind goes on broadcasting them anyway. When you shine a light on your negative thoughts — and see that you don't have to believe in them — it takes away much of their power to create misery.

~ Marci Shimoff, motivational speaker
& author

At one point in my life, I was a divorced mother working full-time to support my two young daughters. Living paycheck to paycheck, I couldn't afford to buy myself health insurance.

When I became very ill, I literally had to drag my body to a free health clinic. A lot of negative thinking went on in my head before I made it to the door of the clinic that day. Embarrassed that I couldn't pay for my medical expenses, I had already convinced myself that when I stepped inside, everyone would look at me like I was a total loser.

I was well dressed in the clothes that I had made, and people would probably think I was taking advantage of the system. Struggling with conflicting feelings about having to accept public assistance and wanting to get well, I swallowed my pride, walked into the clinic, and said that I was sick and needed help.

To my surprise, nothing happened the way I had expected. I was treated like a person who mattered. The nurses and doctors honored the part of me that needed medical attention and validated my worth as a human being. As a result, I walked out of the clinic with a completely different attitude than when I went in.

"Wait a minute," I thought. "I'm not so bad! I'm a working mom doing the best I can." The realization was so uplifting that it could have been as loud as a choir in heaven, but it was more like a quiet angel's whisper, a gentle breeze letting me know that I had all of this amazing potential inside of me. My whole attitude shifted in the blink of an eye! Suddenly, instead of being filled with preconceived notions and negative thoughts, I was filled with radiant hope.

Nothing else changed that day. I still lived in the same house, had the same job, and was still making the same amount of money. But my visit to the clinic changed the direction of my life because that was the moment I decided to change the way I think.

I believe many women have a little place inside our minds where we prejudge ourselves because we don't think we are good enough. Although I didn't realize it at the time, by creating an erroneous idea about how I would be perceived at the clinic, I had set myself up for failure. Sometimes, all it takes is a shift in perspective to turn your life around.

Happiness and success are all about perception and how we deal with the cards we are dealt. The truth is: our reality is constantly shifting from one moment to the next. Life can change on a dime.

I'm not saying that a happy attitude will make everything great, but it can make all the difference in the quality of a day.

~ Cheryl Saban, Ph.D.

Cheryl Saban, Ph.D, psychologist, philanthropist, social activist and author is a dedicated champion for the empowerment of women and the founder of the nonprofit Women's Self Worth Foundation. Her latest book is titled "What is your Self-Worth? A Woman's Guide to Validation." A member of the American Psychological Association, Cheryl is on the Board of Trustees of Children's Hospital of Los Angeles, the Los Angeles Free Clinic and the Mental Health and Research Center at UCLA.

www.whatisyourselfworth.com

Alexia Salvatierra

Struggling for Justice

Becoming a mother makes you a mother of all children. From now on each abandoned, wounded or frightened child is yours. You live in the suffering of mothers of every race   and creed and weep with them. You long to comfort all who are desolate.

~ Charlotte Gray

I am a Lutheran Pastor, and for over thirty years I have been involved in the movement for social justice and civil rights whether it is on behalf of low wage workers, immigrants or the homeless. My work is not just a job—it is my intimate community.

Each battle for justice has given me a deeper understanding of the reason for my existence and has helped me to make sense of my own private struggles. Everything I do is intertwined with what I do and who I am.

Reflecting upon key events that have shaped my life, I realize they are all connected to people who are suffering and striving to build a better world. There is something very universal about being touched by the pain and courage of others if we are able to connect their problems to ours and abstract a message from each one.

Several years ago, my eleven-year-old daughter had been experiencing flu-like symptoms. When she woke up one morning with a high fever and a stiff neck, I took her to the doctor who confirmed my fear. My only child was suffering from meningitis—an excruciatingly painful, viral infection which causes a potentially life-threatening inflammation of the brain and spiral cord. With good health insurance, she was immediately put in the hospital and received excellent medical care.

My daughter's health crisis came at a very poignant time for me. The organization that I directed was just about to kick off a "Week of Walking Prayer" during which faith leaders would publicly support striking grocery workers' fight to maintain health insurance benefits for their families.

I had been planning and organizing this large event for several months. Now, instead of being there to direct my staff in person, I had to speak with them by telephone at the same time I was in the hospital holding and comforting my terrified child as she cried out for me in agony.

My daughter was released from the hospital on the last day of the vigil. She was frail and weak but insisted on going to the grocery store to see the striking workers. When we arrived, she noticed a young boy walking at his mother's side. Turning to me, she asked, "Mommy, if this little boy gets really sick like me, will his Momma be able to take him to the hospital in time so the doctors can save his life too?"

Her innocent question caught me by surprise. That, and the timing of her illness, was a powerful moment of revelation about the motivation that sustains me and people of all faiths in our relentless struggle for justice.

When we truly understand that being one spiritual family under God means that all children are our children, the power of the love that moves us to sacrifice for our own enables us to keep on struggling until all our children are as happy and healthy as they can possibly be.

~ Alexia Salvatierra

Reverend Alexia Salvatierra, an ordained Lutheran Pastor, is a leader in the New Sanctuary Movement dedicated to protecting immigrants against human rights violations. She is the founding director of FaithRooted.org and served as the Executive Director of C.L.U.E. (Clergy and Laity United for Economic Justice.)

www.faithrooted.org

Deborah Santana

Love is the Question and the Answer

In our personal lives empower ourselves with gift values, gratitude, community, turning towards the earth, spirituality. Pay attention to needs. Validate empathy.

~ Genevieve Vaughn, author

I dropped out of college at twenty-one to travel the world with my soon-to-be husband. I had been an English major at a state university with a desire to become a writer or a professor. Instead, I became an expert at maneuvering my way through international airports and visiting museums that held the artworks of masters such as Van Gogh, Dalí, Cassat, and Picasso.

My classroom became bullet trains through the Japanese countryside and tour buses on the streets of Sydney, Rio de Janeiro, and in the South of France.

One summer I volunteered at Family Service Agency to help pre-school teachers. The children came from the neighborhood close by, not an affluent one at all. Sniffling noses, and sleepy eyes greeted me my first morning. With a tissue in hand, I bent down to wipe a little boy's nose, and he recoiled from me as if I were going to strike him.

I still remember the glint of sunlight on his wooly hair, and time stood still as I realized that someone must have hit him. My reaching toward his face had triggered his fearful reaction. My stomach turned over in grief and pain as I kneeled down and asked if I could help him blow his nose. He shyly nodded yes, and then smiled. I wondered how I could make a difference in his life, or even save him from being hit again.

That little boy inspired me to reach out to those who have been hurt in life by living with compassion and helping victims of violence find healing. Each of us is part of the other, the land, the sky, and the future. Everything we do impacts the consciousness of the planet, and moves us closer to peace or to imbalance. The little boy taught me to carry his soft face with me as I travel through the world, remembering that love is the question and the answer.

~ Deborah Santana

Deborah Santana is Founder and CEO of Do A Little, a non-profit that serves women in the areas of health, education, and happiness. She is author of a memoir, "Space Between the Stars: My Journey to an Open Heart", and recently contributed to "Tutu: Authorized." Mother of three beloved young adults, Deborah is a longtime mediator. She did complete her BA, and is studying for a Master's Degree in Women's Spirituality.

http://www.doalittle.org   *www.deborahsantana.com*

Eveline Shen

The Habit of Being

I feel now as if a huge burden has been lifted ... since I have accomplished the most important thing in my life, I am going to enjoy this moment and then think about what I am going to do.

~ Kim Yuna, Olympic Gold Medalist

Six weeks into my paid three-month sabbatical, I became filled with anxiety. "Time is running out," I told a good friend, "and there are about twenty things on my list that I need to do before going back to work!"

When I explained all the things that I hoped to accomplish during the second half of my sabbatical, (which included painting my daughter's room, arranging for music lessons and organizing a local mother-daughter group) my friend looked at me and said, "This is ridiculous! Why did you even write a list? Tear it up right now!" "I can't do that," I replied. "Having a list is the way I run my life."

My friend encouraged me to think about the reasons why I was given a sabbatical. "After eleven years of dedicated leadership," she said, "your Board of Directors wanted to recognize the outstanding job you have done. Your sabbatical was meant to be a gift so you could connect with family and friends and have some time for yourself. Your Board wants you to come back feeling refreshed and rejuvenated, not frazzled and frustrated."

What she said was true. For many months I had been literally running from one meeting to the next in my demanding career. Working on a new national project, my hours had increased dramatically. All at once it hit me. I had created a very similar high-pressured, high-productivity, high-accountability environment at home.

The list of things to do during my sabbatical had become a huge burden on my shoulders. I hadn't realized how much stress I had created for myself. It was a surprise to realize that I had been judging my self-worth on my habits of doing instead of on the habit of being — giving myself time to be still and to just be me.

Later that evening, I tore up my list. I thought about the things that were most important to me and what I wanted the core of my life to be about. On the top of the page of a new piece of paper I wrote: Meaning, Community, Joy. The next few days were spent reflecting upon the different pathways that would take me in the direction I wanted to go.

I came to understand that real self-worth can never measured by what I do. It is based upon a deep inner appreciation for my unique presence in the world and knowing that I can reach my potential as a human being. For me, this moment of revelation was as refreshing as jumping into cool water on a hot summer day.

The next six weeks were spent unwinding, enjoying my family and connecting with friends. When my sabbatical was over, I was in a very different place emotionally, spiritually, and physically. I had become a stronger and more well-grounded woman. Refreshed and rejuvenated, I was ready to go back to work.

~ Eveline Shen

Eveline Shen is the Executive Director of Forward Together, a Woman's Foundation of California grant partner that leads grass roots actions and trains community leaders to transform policy and culture in ways that support individuals, families and communities to reach their full potential. A Gerbode Fellow, Eveline was named one of Women's e-News' Twenty-One Leaders for the Twenty-First Century.

www.forwardtogether.org

Lateefah Simon

Finding My Power

The most common way people give up their power is by thinking they don't have any.

~Alice Walker, author

I was in a state of denial when, four months out of high school, a friend remarked that I looked pregnant. Wanting to prove her wrong, I stopped by an organization called the Homeless Prenatal Project and told a young African-American case manager that I needed to take a pregnancy test. "My name is Sabrina," the woman said. "After you take the test, let's sit down and talk."

When the result came back positive, I panicked and cried: "This can't be true. I'm only eighteen. This is not a good time! Nothing in my life is right. I graduated high school by the skin of my teeth. I'm living with my mother in low-income housing, and I only work ten hours a week. I can't afford to take care of a baby. I don't want to be an unwed mother! What am I going to do?"

That's when I heard the words that transformed my life:

You have a number of options. But whatever you do and whatever you decide, know that you are going to come out of this stronger. I believe in the power of women, and I believe in your power. I know you will make the choice that is right for you.

Sabrina wasn't judging me. She wasn't preaching. She was like an angel who appeared in what could have been my darkest hour. Her message wasn't just about a women's right to reproductive freedom. This was about another woman looking me in the eye and saying that I had the ability to control my destiny one-hundred percent. Until that moment I never actually understood that I had complete power over my own life!

I went home and made what was for me, a deeply profound decision: I would have the baby and raise it on my own. This wasn't a popular choice at the time, but I thought that if another woman could believe in my power, then I should start to believe in it too.

After I broke the news to my mother, I promised that she wouldn't have to take care of me and my child. "I want to take care of you," she insisted. "I want to take care of you and your baby." Strangely enough, our relationship blossomed, and we became closer than we had ever been. When my daughter was born, my mother fell in love with her first grandchild, and she helped me parent my little girl.

Fifteen years later, I take Sabrina's message with me wherever I go. Her words helped me to find my place in the world as a single mother and shaped what I hope will be a long career as an advocate for young women and girls who, for whatever reason, have ended up homeless and involved in sex trafficking and drugs.

After all, if I hadn't met a woman named Sabrina, I might never have known that it is very possible to turn pain into power and come out better and stronger on the other side.

~ Lateefah Simon

Lateefah Simon, a respected civil rights leader, serves as the Director of the Rosenberg Foundation's California's Future initiative, a strategic effort to change the odds for women and children statewide. Lateefah, named California's Woman of the Year by the California State Assembly in 2005, has received numerous awards including the MacArthur "Genius" Fellowship and the Jefferson Award for extraordinary public service.

www.rosenbergfound.org

Valerie Sobel

A Planet of Our Own

That inner voice has both gentleness and clarity. So, to get to authenticity, you really need to keep going down to the bone, to the honesty, and the inevitability of something.

~Meredith Monk, singer & composer

Perhaps it would not have been possible for me to seek or to find God without the urgency of tragedy. The life I knew collapsed when my seventeen-year-old son was diagnosed with an inoperable, malignant brain tumor. Suddenly stricken with double vision, this exquisitely different, absolutely brilliant child became blind. A few months later, he lost his ability to speak.

With every fiber of my being I wanted to protect my child and be by his side every minute of the 417 days of his grave illness caring for him and loving him. Nothing mattered except spending time with my son.

Practicing religious ritual and being obedient to the law of a Higher Power is not the same as praying for a child's life. For months I alternated between praying on my knees for a miracle, to surrendering with "I will to will Thy will," to trusting God, to feeling abandoned. Times like this take you down to the bone and provide a glimpse of what real faith must be like.

In that place of mystery beyond human ability to define what is good or bad, all the masks melted away leaving only pure love. This enormous untainted love put Andre and me on a planet of our own, somewhere not of this world. I was Mother as never before, and in a way I hope to never be again.

It was essential that I honor Andre's life. I donated money in his memory, bought gifts for needy children and worked with teenagers living on the streets or under bridges, young people who had either run away from home or were rejected by their parents. I became a CASA, a Court Appointed Special Advocate, in the juvenile delinquency system in an attempt to find my cause. It took five years to happen upon my mission, suddenly and unexpectedly, as if in the blink of an eye.

At a New Year's millennium party, feeling somewhat alienated, I withdrew to another room and prayed to be given the direction that I had been desperately seeking. The still, small voice inside me said, "If you are going to get on with your life, what is the one thing that you know with absolute certainty?" *I knew what it was like to be the mother of a dying child!* In a burst of clarity I understood exactly what my purpose was.

It wasn't Andre's life that I needed to honor — it was the time we spent together. I suddenly realized how fortunate I was compared to some of the other mothers that I met during my son's treatment. I couldn't let go of a particular memory of a twelve-year-old boy in the next room. He had cancer too but was alone. When I asked why, he said, "My mom works and needs to take care of my brothers and sisters."

This mother had to leave her child alone, unable to do the thing she wanted most to do: comfort and be with him during his last days. I didn't have to choose between staying at the hospital and going to work to pay medical bills and insurance or to keep food on the table. I could afford to stay at my child's side to the day of his death. My time with Andre wasn't diluted for a second.

Filled with gratitude for my privileges and blessings, I realized that what I was being called to do was bigger than Andre and I. It has been said, "When the student is ready, the teacher appears." All alone in that quiet room, I picked up a book and happened upon a quote that changed my life:

Whatever you can do, or dream you can do, begin it. Boldness has genius, power and magic in it. (Johann Wolfgang von Goethe)

It is a mystery why the deepest truths are revealed in the midst of great hardships and sorrow. But on the eve of the millennium, I had found the right way to honor the gift of time that I had with my dying son: helping other mothers to experience the real, authentic moments we had shared, moments that no one ever really thinks or talks about.

Providence moves through us when we seek our purpose and trust that the right answer will come in its own time and in its own way.

~ Valerie Sobel

Valerie Sobel is the founder and president of the Andre River of Life Foundation, a national nonprofit organization enabling single caregivers of children with life threatening illness to care for them full time by relieving financial burdens when other resources are exhausted or unavailable. She is a recognized speaker on the subject of caregiver support, a charter member of the Women of Washington/Los Angeles, and a founding member of the Women's Foundation of California's Donor Circle.

www.andreriveroflife.org

Jackie Speier

A Second Lease on Life

Life is not a matter of milestones, but of moments.
~Rose Fitzgerald Kennedy

In 1978 I was a twenty-eight year old congressional staffer on an ill-fated fact-finding trip in Guyana, South America. Our mission was to investigate allegations that the People's Temple Christian Church was holding American citizens against their will.

Congressman Leo Ryan led the delegation to the church's jungle commune where members, relatives of Representative Ryan's constituents, said they were subjected to brutal beatings. There were rumors of murders and a mass suicide plan that later came to pass — tragically over 900 people, many of them children, were either poisoned or shot to death. After a twenty-four hour stay in Jonestown, we left quickly after an attempt was made on the Congressman's life.

Many people wanted to leave the commune, and I was helping to load them on a plane when a tractor-trailer appeared out of nowhere. Unbeknownst to us, we had been followed. All at once seven gunmen began shooting mostly at point blank range. Representative Ryan, who was shot forty-five times, became the only member of Congress to be killed in the line of duty. Four other people died as well. I was shot five times and left for dead.

"Oh My God!" I thought. "This is it! I'm not going to live eighty-plus years. I'm not going to have children and live happily ever after. None of these things are going to happen for me." Lying on a remote airstrip for twenty-two hours without medical attention, bleeding and covered by ants, it was devastating to think that my life would end this way.

In retrospect, this horrific experience was an opportunity to reorder and reassess my life. On the airstrip I decided that if I did survive, I would never take another day for granted. I would live each moment as fully as possible, and I would commit my life to public service. After being rescued and enduring two long months in the hospital, ten surgeries, and three years of physical therapy to regain my strength, I went out and fulfilled my promise.

My second lease on life was a great gift. It has made me fearless. I had looked at death in the eye and survived. There was no reason to be afraid of the wounds that left a multitude of scars over my body. I was alive.

~ Jackie Speier

Jackie Speier is the U.S. Representative for California's 12th congressional district serving since 2008 and a former member of the California State Senate. In more than eighteen years in the California State Assembly and Senate, she has authored over 300 bills that were signed into law by both Democratic and Republican governors. Jackie is also co-author of the best-selling book, "This is Not the Life I Ordered: 50 Ways to Keep Your Head Above Water When Life Keeps Dragging You Down."

Anne Stockwell

Flooded with Joy

My cancer scare changed my life. I'm grateful for every new, healthy day I have. It has helped me prioritize my life.

~Olivia Newton-John

Everyone faces adversity in their own way. When I was diagnosed with ovarian cancer over ten years ago, I experienced it as a wake-up call to celebrate all the reasons why I was put on earth.

I had been feeling more tired than usual. But I'd also been working very long days, so I didn't believe anything was wrong—until one night I experienced the gift of a strange abdominal pain. The pain wasn't terrible, just odd. It would have been easy to ignore. Yet some instinct told me to see a doctor. That gift of pain, so rare with ovarian cancer, is why I'm alive today.

A whirlwind of tests at the hospital produced results that I could barely comprehend. Even the ultrasound technician looked grim. He said, "Let's prepare for the worst and hope for the best." I was in shock. Me? Cancer? No way!

Then the blood test they call a "tumor marker" came back 800 times too high. And I realized: It's true. I have cancer.

In the next moment, the most surprising thing happened. A flood of pure joy washed over me—a sensation of bliss unlike anything I had ever experienced. Just like in the movies, my entire life flashed before my eyes. I saw—I felt!—how blessed I was to have been born with so many talents and so many opportunities to use them. In a nanosecond, I relived music and films I'd made and my career as a journalist at a groundbreaking magazine. I remembered people I had loved, people who loved me. I saw so clearly: I had made a difference!

I knew that if this was the end, I could depart well-satisfied. Yet I also knew: If it was not my time to go, I could move forward appreciating the gift of life in a deeper, more meaningful way.

I sent out this simple wish to the universe: "I love my life! I want more!"

As of 2012, I've gotten my wish ten times over. It hasn't always been easy. After my first surgery and chemotherapy, my cancer returned twice. But so what? Here I am. And I can honestly say that none of my treatment on any given day was unbearable. Nothing was as bad as I feared. Each time, my doctors have had more effective tools to help me. And each year, science comes closer to confirming what I already know: Joy heals.

Through my unique experience, my next career is taking shape. I want to communicate the gifts of joy, gratitude, and wonder to other people facing great personal adversity.

I have never lost the exuberance that cancer unlocked for me— the thrill of waking up every morning and realizing that whatever the day might bring, the good, the bad, and everything in-between, it is all a glorious gift. With a positive attitude, we can transcend adversity, be transformed by it, and go on to prosper and thrive.

~ Anne Stockwell

Anne Stockwell is an author, editor, filmmaker, and illustrator. Her book "The Guerrilla Guide to Mastering Student Loan Debt" was a groundbreaking manual for dealing with the student loan industry. She co-founded MoneyPants.com, a pop-influenced, personal-finance site for women. Anne was with The Advocate magazine for fifteen years as an editor and editor in chief. Currently she is the founder of WellAgain.org, a service community dedicated to helping cancer survivors rejoin the adventure of living.

www.WellAgain.org

Marilyn Tam

Making a Difference

How wonderful it is that nobody need wait a single moment before starting to improve the world.

~Anne Frank

I rushed through my undergraduate and graduate studies in four years in order to fulfill a life-long dream: working for the World Health Organization. I envisioned that working with them would allow me to fulfill my life mission of making a difference as soon as possible. The response to my application was a form letter saying they only hired people with ten years of experience.

At the age of twenty-one, it felt as if my whole career had blown away before I even got started! Re-centering myself, I took a deep breath and thought, "I still want to make a big impact on the world as soon as possible. What else can I do?" The answer that came to me was to get a job at a bank. Working with money, I reasoned, can make change happen quickly. If you control the money, you can control how resources are allocated.

I applied to the biggest bank around knowing that I was more than qualified. The executive training positions required a bachelor's degree; I had a Masters in economics. But after going through the interviewing process, I did not get any kind of response until I finally talked to one of the men who had interviewed me. After a lot of hemming and hawing, he said, "We don't hire women as executive trainees."

A sad and very familiar feeling came over me when I heard these words. Born into a very traditional family in Hong Kong in the 1950's, I had the misfortune of being the second daughter of Chinese parents desperate for a son. Dirt was more valuable than a useless girl. "Dear God," I thought. "Will it ever be possible to achieve my dream of making a difference? Will I always be judged by my gender instead of the person I am?"

The two places where I wanted to start my career shut their doors to me. Devastated, I had to step back and think, "What can I do now with what I have?" Well, I still have my education and my passion to make a difference, those things can never be taken away. This forced me to think even harder and ask myself, "Am I going to let outside circumstances stop me? Or am I going to work through this and succeed?"

I decided to visit the university admissions office and research career opportunities for students transitioning into the business world. Looking at the different jobs available, it hit me: I didn't need a grandiose plan to change the world right then and there. The realization I had at that moment was—I *don't have to wait! I can make a difference now*—no matter where I end up!

After interviewing with the recruiter of a large department store, and knowing nothing about retail, I discovered that I had found an organization with a planned system in place to grade and promote people based on their performance regardless of gender or color. This was quite a revelation! Still, when they offered me a job, I went through the difficult process of debating if I was giving up my dream by working for this company.

I realized that I had been trying to fit my image into something that was not my reality at that time. I needed to shift my expectations and say, "I know that I can achieve! Here is a place that will judge me on my merits. This is where I can use my assets, my training and my passion to make a difference *now*!"

My unexpected career in retail was launched by opening my mind to new possibilities. Going forward, I leveraged whatever I could do into making a difference in all the things I have done. If one door closes, I always look for another door, or a window, to go through. There is no good reason to wait. Do something positive with your life … *now*!

~ Marilyn Tam

Marilyn Tam, *Ph.D. is a Speaker, Author, Consultant, Founder and Executive Director of Us Foundation. She was formerly the CEO of Aveda Corp., President of Reebok Apparel and Retail Group; Vice President of Nike Inc. Her book, "How to Use What You've Got to Get What You Want", is in six languages. Her new book, "Living the Life of Your Dreams" won as eBook of the Year 2011 in the Inspirational/Visionary category.*

www.MarilynTam.com

Hiroko Tatebe

Finding My Unique Worth

...the heart doesn't lie. Nor does the heart change. What changes are our feelings.

~Higuchi Ichiyo, first modern professional
Japanese woman writer

I always wanted to be in a position where I could make my own choices. It wouldn't be easy for a girl born into a male-dominated society ruled by rigid Japanese cultural expectations and traditional values. When I grew up in downtown Tokyo, women were only recognized as someone's wife, mother or daughter, not as a separate person with her own unique worth.

Raised with five older sisters in a close-knit community, I was a sickly child unable to attend kindergarten. When I finally received permission to enter first grade, I was very excited. My whole world opened up! Playing with other children was the start of my life-long appreciation for building strong relationships.

In elementary school, it was fun to be me, Hiroko, rather than the sixth Tatebe daughter or someone's little sister. But the cultural expectations for girls and women were always there forcing me to behave in clearly defined ways. Believing that one day I would be free, I only pretended to play the traditional roles.

Sadly, freedom came at the age of sixteen when my father, chairman of a savings and loan company, passed away and my mother was elected as a director of the bank. It was extremely rare for a Japanese woman to be given such an important position in those days, but my mother was different. With numerous professional connections and high social standing, my mother was far ahead of her time.

Her success proved what could happen if a woman was given a fair opportunity and was willing to work hard. My mother's new career helped her to understand my burning need for independence, and she agreed to let me get my college education in the United States.

After graduation I got a job in Southern California at a Japanese bank. Like my parents, I climbed the corporate ladder as Director, Executive Vice President, and Treasurer. I most enjoyed my role as a liaison between Japan and America until I turned fifty. I realized that I wanted to do more than be a banker and left the bank.

At the same time, my mother became gravely ill, and I went to Japan to spend time with her. After she died, I was no longer anyone's daughter. I no longer had my former banking titles. I realized it is so easy to define ourselves by the different roles we play and then feel lost when they are gone. That's when a little voice told me to look inside my heart, and in that quiet moment of self-reflection, I found my unique worth.

I saw myself as a little girl playing with friends and maturing into a young woman who dreamed about making choices. I loved bringing people together and serving as a liaison between my two countries. My unique worth could be realized by building a bridge of understanding between the women of America and Japan!

Many women around the world can only dream about the freedom that we are privileged to have. Every person deserves a chance to succeed, but many people don't know how or where to begin. Little by little, working together, we can make a big difference.

Listen to the message in your heart. Always remember that real success has little to do with roles or titles—and everything to do with realizing your own unique worth.

~ Hiroko Tatebe

Hiroko Tatebe is the founder of (GOLD) Global Organization for Leadership & Diversity and a founding member of (GEWEL) Global Enhancement of Women's Executive Leadership based in Japan. Her passion is to build leadership bridges across the Pacific. She is active in many organizations such as the Multicultural Board of the Women's Leadership Exchange, Big Thinking Women, and the Japan America Society. Hiroko has received many awards and honors including Outstanding Business Woman of the Year.

www.goldleaders.org

Gayle Tauber

Living Outside the Box

Certain springs are tapped only when we are alone. The artist knows he must be alone to create; the writer to work out his thoughts; the musician to compose; the saint, to pray. But women need solitude in order to find again the true essence of themselves.

~Anne Morrow Lindberg

For as long as I can remember, I put myself in a box and sealed it with a label that read, "a shy, reserved, conservative, behind-the-scenes person lives inside—definitely not a risk-taker, certainly not a leader." I imagined myself labeled that way for most of my life.

As a young woman, I saw myself as an adult walking briskly and carrying a brief case. No thought was given as to where I was going or what was inside the briefcase. I just connected carrying one to finding a positive, acceptable place for myself in the world. I was a high achiever, but at the same time, I thought that I was someone who preferred the "known" to the "unknown," someone who needed to be in control of her life experiences. I continued to frame myself within that image even as a mature woman.

By the end of my college years, I had moved out of my family's home into marriage, and with my business-partner-husband, rolled into one entrepreneurial start-up business after another while raising two daughters. Somehow, in between, I was able to grab rare slivers of time for myself.

My journey was focused outward, a common path I shared with other women. It wasn't until I turned fifty-two and sold our last business that I had the luxury of solitude for deep personal reflection. Taking time to examine myself apart from my career, I discovered that honest self-appraisal can provide direction and intent when needed most.

My garden became a safe place where I found the comfort and serenity necessary for deep reflection. Here was the opportunity to think about where I had been, who I was, and where I wanted to go next. Digging into the soil and nurturing my roses were life-changing moments of self-discovery and personal awareness. Working alone among the flowers in my beautiful garden and enjoying the ocean breezes, I was able to see myself as I really am.

Much to my surprise, I realized that I had never been that person in the box after all! My revelation was that I had not recognized all the positive, unusual things I had done in my life. In fact, I had lived life as a risk-taker, a visionary, a philanthropist, and a mother—not as the shy, conservative person that I thought I was.

I never stopped to acknowledge my success in starting national and international businesses where I took upfront visible leads and made executive decisions that impacted the direction of our companies and affected the well-being of many others. I never identified these accomplishments as the result of leading a more risk prone life.

It was surprising to realize that I had been giving, taking, experiencing and stretching all along—far beyond what I perceived my limits were and never really understanding that I wasn't afraid of the unknown. The truth was—I thrived on it! Even when I stumbled, I was able to right myself for the next new adventure, learning and growing from lessons learned along the way.

After much soul-searching, I decided that the next chapter of my life would be about stretching beyond my comfort zone even further. I wanted to continue to grow as a human being and experience the full richness of life. Knowing that all I had to do was just get out of my own way gave me confidence to ramp it up even more. The awareness of my own truth was freeing and exhilarating!

Unless you take time to examine yourself deeply and carefully, it is possible to go through life not knowing your innate capabilities or understanding how to fully blossom into your unique self. Solitude and contemplation are gifts that bring clarity and truth.

What picture have you framed of you? Where is your life headed? Is that where you want to go? What sacrifices will you make in negotiating your path? What labels do you wear? Are they self or other-attributed? Do these labels bring you to your own truth?

Plunging my hands into the soil, these are questions I still ask myself. Setting aside time for personal reflection is a part of my journey now. Nurturing my flowers and my soul in peaceful solitude, I dig deeper and deeper into the essence of the woman I am.

~ Gayle Tauber

Gayle Tauber is a cofounder of the Kashi Company, later sold to the Kellogg Company; currently, she is CEO of Seedling Fund, a family investment company. Gayle, involved in entrepreneurial business focusing on health/wellness, social responsibility and the preservation of capital, is a cofounder of Women Give San Diego, past president of The Trusteeship, the Southern California chapter of the International Women's Foundation and former board member of the Women's Foundation of California.

Stacy Tilliss

The One in Control

In giving language to my experience, I hope I can make rape less 'unspeakable.' I hope to dispel at least some part of the fear and shame that has made victims mute.

~Nancy Raine, author

At the tender age of fifteen, I learned a powerful lesson — that I will always have absolute control over my life, no matter how terrifying the situation, and no matter how powerless someone else tries to make me feel.

When I was growing up, my parents had a second home in Palm Springs, and we went to the desert every weekend. As a child I loved to go with them, but when I hit my teenage years, it was more important to be with my friends. Staying at my cousins' beach house was what I really wanted to do, and I always had an open invitation.

My parents agreed to let me go every now and then until one night a horrific incident occurred. Asleep in the guest room, I was awakened in the middle of the night by the sound of someone or something rummaging through my suitcase on the floor nearby. Thinking it was a dog or a cat, I suddenly remembered that my cousins didn't have any pets. At about 3:30 am, a different kind of animal had broken into the house.

Pretending to sleep, I prayed the intruder would just take whatever he wanted and leave. But then a two hundred and fifty pound man approached my bed wielding a very large machete-like knife. Holding the blade at my side, and trying to prove to a fifteen year old girl that she was not in control of the situation, he raped me.

Something inside me said, "Do not lose your life over this. Turn the situation around. Become the one in control." Treating my attacker as if he were someone I cared for, I calmly said, "My purse is on the other side of the bed. Take my money and my father's credit card which I use in an emergency while he is away. Something awful must have happened to make you do this. I'm sorry you have lost your path in life, and I want to help you find it again." I gave him my telephone number and told him to call whenever he needed to talk.

Before leaving, my rapist instructed me to stay in bed for ten minutes. It was the longest ten minutes of my life. During the rape, I pretended I wasn't even in the room, but staring at the clock and counting each second, the nightmare I had just experienced became very real. Completely traumatized at the ten-minute mark, I got up and ran to my cousins who took me to the hospital.

A few weeks later, my attacker called not knowing the phone lines were tapped or that his voice was being taped for identification. I kept encouraging him to use my dad's credit card. When he finally used it at a gas station, the police were notified with his location. He was immediately arrested. After I testified at his trial, he was sent to prison.

The people at the Santa Monica rape treatment center made all the difference in my recovery. I can't recall very much about the therapy I received; I only remember being helped and supported by many caring people. I know my healing experiences in the treatment center were the beginning of a journey that brought me to where I am today: a wife and a proud mother of a daughter and son.

Being a victim of rape is not something I would ever wish on anyone. Bad things really can happen to good people. But no matter how scary a situation, and no matter how powerless another person tries to make you feel, just remember that you are always in control of every moment of your life too.

~ Stacy Tilliss

Stacy Tilliss *has been happily married to her high school sweetheart for over twenty-four years. She is currently a full-time wife and mother to a son and daughter. Stacy is an active volunteer in her local temple and contributes her time and energy to many other nonprofit organizations in the community.*

Helen Torres

The Spirit of Advocacy

I stand on the shoulders of countless people, yet there is one extraordinary person who is my life aspiration – that person is my mother ...

~Sonia Sotomayor

I still remember the overwhelming feeling of anxiety and fear when the airplane hit the ground and landed in America. A three year old immigrant child from Puerto Rico, I reached out to my mother for comfort and instantly knew everything would be okay.

People in our new suburban community found it difficult to understand my mother's thick Spanish accent. In elementary school some of the other mothers would snicker and correct her choice of words, and their children made fun of my mom's broken English. Understanding that "fitting in" and establishing a sense of community for her two daughters was important to my mother, I became very protective of her, as she was of my sister and me.

A particular incident in third grade haunts me to this day. My mother received a phone call from another mother asking her to bring cupcakes to a school event. My mom didn't understand exactly what the woman was asking for. She baked a beautiful cake, and on the day of the event we were proud to take our contribution to school.

The woman ridiculed my mother when she saw the cake. "I didn't ask for a cake! I asked for cupcakes! Don't you even know what cupcakes are? When are you going to learn how to speak English?" Not only did the woman humiliate my mother, she embarrassed me in front of my peers. Because her language and accent were being attacked, my mother didn't say a single word. Silently, she looked at the rude woman and stood her ground.

"My mother speaks two languages," I cried out in her defense. "Why can't you see that she is really trying? Besides, this is a beautiful cake!" The woman was embarrassed to be reprimanded by an angry third-grader, and as much as my mother tried to assure me that everything was fine, the tears in her eyes said otherwise. I saw a little piece of her soul disappear that day, and although she continued her political activism and community involvement, my mother never volunteered at school again.

I have carried this moment with me through all the important transitions in my life. In retrospect, defending my mother was the seed that gave rise to the spirit of advocacy that would eventually put me on the path to becoming a voice for women who are like mothers and sisters to me. Looking out for them speaks to the essence of who I am and who I am still becoming.

~ Helen Torres

Helen Torres is the Executive Director and CEO of HOPE (Hispanics Organized for Political Equality), a non-profit, non-partisan women's organization committed to ensuring political and economic parity for Latinas and advocating for Latina representation as decision-makers and community leaders statewide. She serves on CaliforniaVolunteers Commission and the ZeroDivide Foundation board. Helen and her husband, Jonathan, are proud parents to Adam and Joshua.

Anne Smith Towbes

A Bit of Wisdom

Courage doesn't always roar. Sometimes courage is the quiet voice at the end of the day saying, "I will try again tomorrow."

~Mary Anne Radmacher

Before moving to California over twenty years ago, I gained a bit of wisdom from an elderly black woman who was passing out samples of a new type of soup in a local grocery store right in the middle of a raging Michigan blizzard. Having trudged over five freezing blocks in foot high snow to buy some groceries, I was stunned to see her there.

I learned that she had ridden a bus from downtown Detroit to get to her job. The ride must have taken hours to arrive at the suburb where I was living. I couldn't believe this remarkable woman actually made it to work in such terrible weather!

When she noticed my surprise, the woman said, "Darlin,' you just can't let your fear getcha because if you do, it will only grow!"

From that very brief encounter, I learned that sometimes you just have to keep trudging along in life — one slow and slushy footstep at a time.

The philosophy of putting one foot forward at a time and not letting "your fear getcha" helped me immeasurably when my family and I moved to California. A few years later, my husband of thirty-two years began to experience stomach problems. After a CAT Scan revealed a large tumor on his liver, he stoically announced that he was going to die.

In that moment I decided that fear would not get in my way. I'd just have to deal with my husband's illness and his complicated all-consuming treatment one step at a time. And that is exactly what I did. My husband remained positive and upbeat, so he also reflected this philosophy. It wasn't easy, but we held our heads high and kept trudging along just like the courageous woman in the grocery store.

I'm sure this sweet lady doesn't remember me, but I will never forget her. I often think back with gratitude for her inspiring words that helped me to face my husband's passing with strength and dignity. Even today her simple but profound message still defines my reaction to life's challenges.

~ Anne Smith Towbes

Anne Smith Towbes taught English and Drama to students in grades 4-12 for the first twenty years of her professional life. Ms. Towbes is a former Trustee of the Santa Barbara Foundation and the Hutton Foundation. She was president of the Lobero Theater and is currently on the board of KDB, the local classical radio station. Her telethons on KEYT-TV, which she owns through Smith Media, support the Unity Shoppe, Cottage Shoppe and Mission for Mentors.

Jan Tuttleman

Message in a Dream

Dreams are illustrations ... from the book your soul is writing about you.

~Marsha Norman, American playwright

Several years ago, over the course of about six months, I began having a series of three dreams that were very disturbing. My dreams upset me so much that I decided to enroll in a dream interpretation class hoping to gain some insight into what it all meant.

In the first dream I was failing out of college and graduate school. In the real world I already had a Masters and Ph.D., but in the dream I was filled with great anxiety about not being able to finish my education. It struck me as odd that the classes were always in Humanities when I had actually studied science.

My second dream was about a man who I found to be extremely attractive. Happily married, it was unsettling to think that subconsciously I wanted to be married to someone else. In the last dream I was always going through long, narrow, and winding tunnels where I was overcome with claustrophobia.

The night before the class, I had one dream in which all three components came together. I was failing out of college not knowing if I would graduate; then the attractive man appeared and offered to help me figure out what was going on. "Let's go to the registrar's office together," he said reaching his hand out to guide me, "and talk to an advisor."

The man and I went through several small narrow hallways before going up an enormous escalator. At the top of the escalator we encountered what seemed like an endless series of large expansions until finally I saw myself entering a hospital. Somehow, I ended up in a doorway where my husband was standing. On one side of him stood a nurse holding a baby wrapped in a blue blanket.

It happened to be during a time in my life when I had been thinking about having another child, so this dream made sense. "That's it!" I thought. "My dream is about having another baby! I already have two girls. Here is the little boy I've always wanted."

I started the class as planned, and the first assignment was to draw a picture of my dream. When the instructor looked at what I had drawn—me holding a baby in a blue blanket with my arm extended forward reaching out to a man for help, she said, "It isn't a man that you are reaching out to. It is the masculine part of you. The baby represents rebirth and renewal, a symbol of your spiritual awareness." "No! That is not it!" I said astounded at my sudden revelation. "That is not it at all!"

The dream was not about my spiritual awareness—it was about not having a relationship with God. In that moment I was stunned to realize that the attractive man helping me in my dream was not another human being. He was a higher spiritual being.

I never really knew very much about my Jewish religion, but the message in my dream changed the direction and purpose of my life. I decided to learn more about my faith and got involved with a wonderful group of dedicated women who raised money for the local Jewish Federation. I began to practice yoga meditation. Shortly after that, I left a successful career in science and devoted my time to my family and to serving others.

Ten months later my husband passed away unexpectedly in the middle of the night. Suddenly I was a young widow with two little daughters ages three and five. I don't know what I would have done if I hadn't taken the time to discover the message in my dream which ultimately lead me to God and to a community of women who supported me and my daughters as we grieved the loss of a beloved husband and father.

Since that happened, I always listen to my heart. Whenever a door opens, I never hesitate to walk through it.

~ Jan Tuttleman

Jan Tuttleman, former vice president of marketing for Huya Bioscience International, is the chairwoman of the board of the Jewish Federation of San Diego and president and co-owner of Women Give San Diego. She serves on the boards of the Jewish Community Foundation of San Diego, the Sanford-Burnham Institute for Medical Research, the Foundation for Women, the San Diego Jewish Women's Foundation, and the Dean's Advisory Council of the UCSD Rady School of Management.

Note: A few months after sharing her spiritual story, Jan was diagnosed with a malignant brain tumor, Stage IV glioblastoma. She is recovering well in large part due to her spirituality and the love of family and friends. Jan is meeting her tumor head-on, moment to moment, one breath at a time.

Nicole Vazquez

A Dream in My Pocket

I have great faith in the power of women who will dedicate themselves wholeheartedly to the task of remaking our society ... new communities, new cities, a new nation. Yea, a new world which we desperately need!

~Coretta Scott King

My mother was glowing and there was an absolute bounce in her step. She smiled and waved as we walked toward one another on the middle of the hill in our old neighborhood. Such a familiar place and such astounding, life-altering news!

A senior in high school, I had just gotten off the school bus in our gritty urban community near downtown Los Angeles. Mom met me at the bus stop almost every day because she didn't want me to walk home alone. But on that sunny afternoon the look on her face was different from any expression I had ever seen before. I wasn't exactly sure what it meant. I just knew it was good.

My heart soared when my mother placed a large white envelope in my hands—my first letter of acceptance from a four-year university! It was the moment that I had been waiting for. All my hard work had paid off! Instinctively, I understood that life would never be the same again. Nothing changes a person's world like a good education.

Mom was a single parent receiving welfare and raising two daughters in a crime-ridden neighborhood where it wasn't unusual for girls to become pregnant by the age of twelve or thirteen. My mother always did her best to make sure her children performed well in school, so this letter was as much her success as it was mine. The look of pride on my mom's face is something I'll never forget. Thinking about it still brings tears to my eyes.

I was an awkward teenager and a straight "A" student, hopeful and confident in my ability, but unsure about how I could get to my future. Growing up in a neighborhood surrounded by violence, gangs and drugs, life didn't hold very much promise for a girl with a dream in her pocket. People laughed when they heard that I wanted to attend a prestigious university. They made me wonder if my vision of doing something important in the world would ever come true.

I wrote my college application essays in the only bathroom in our small apartment with the toilet as my chair and a TV tray as my desk long after my mother and sister went to bed. Until that first letter of acceptance, I was never exactly sure what the results of my painstaking efforts to get into a top school would actually yield. It was a huge boost of confidence when other acceptance letters followed!

I decided to attend Stanford University, one of the greatest gifts I could have been given, but after graduation I learned that education is a life-long and limitless journey that never ends. My eyes were opened to the full abundance of life—music, poetry, literature, art, fashion, travelling, meeting new people, and most of all, a rewarding career, rooted in passion, that serves the community.

A whole new world was waiting for me! At the same time I realized that education can mean transcendence from poverty, hopelessness and despair. The soaring feeling of pride that I experienced when my mother placed that large white envelope in my hands inspires me to provide opportunities to the many other people who have a dream in their pocket too. We are never too young or too old to better ourselves and the world we share.

~ Nicole Vazquez

Nicole Vazquez is the incoming Board Chair of the Women's Foundation of California and serves as a Principal Consultant to the California State Assembly Budget Committee. She is a recipient of the Cindy Marano Leadership Award from the Women's Policy Institute and the Fierce Warrior Award from the County Welfare Directors Association of California. Nicole began her career as a John Gardner Public Service Fellow.

Louise Jane Wannier

A Sudden Revelation

Art is when you hear a knocking from your soul — and you answer

~Terri Guillemets, anthropologist

Being fired as CEO of the company I started was a horrible blow to my ego. I had been building a business filled with the excitement of trying to create a solution for what I saw as a fashion problem for women and proving my own self worth at the same time. But the company needed more investment capital money in a challenging economy, and my venture investors weren't happy.

The blow to my ego felt like a mortal wound. Getting fired was the perfect stopping point to take stock of where I was in my life and figure out where I wanted to go. I responded by signing up for an intensive eight-day program to assist people who are "ready for a change." This was the beginning of my inner journey, a journey I had always insisted I didn't need because I thought I had already understood myself.

During those eight days I reflected upon the patterns of my life and tried to understand how they had gotten me to the point of being fired from my own company. In the process I learned that most of my life had been about pleasing other people instead of focusing on my happiness. The startling discovery that I was not in alignment with who I am inside as a person was a shock down to the roots of my being!

This was the first step in understanding my true self. It would take time for all the pieces to come together, and it happened when I woke up one morning with a sudden revelation. My former explorations into product development and building companies were only outward projections of my inner drive to create something that didn't exist. It is hard to explain but a feeling of calmness came over me - and in the quiet moment between dream and reality, I knew which way I wanted to go.

I realized that I am a woman who cares deeply about the world, someone who needs to express herself in a wide range of arts and creation. I no longer felt the need to define myself by a particular role or title. Instead, I found peace in knowing that the next part of my journey would be about moving more gently with the flow of life.

The energy and light in nature have always fascinated me. I love the shadows and patterns! My grandfather was a textile merchant from Eastern Europe, and there are tailors on both sides of my family. Textiles and cloth were always part of my childhood. But how could I put all these things together in a kind of paradox that would make a meaningful contribution to the planet and bring my own unique light into the world?

Creating a collection of wearable art scarves became my source of connection to life's spirit to re-energize and re-emerge in new directions. For me, these scarves come to life whenever I see them in connection with other people, and I feel myself connecting from the color and feel of the textiles to the core of my inner spirit, my intuitive essence.

It became clear that that I needed to let go of what other people thought and just be me. I would go forward leading from my heart in a spirit of creativity and vitality rather than purely intellect and ego. Sometimes things take time to percolate, but if you pay attention, the answers will emerge. Within each of us is an amazing inner journey back to simply being ourselves.

~ Louise Jane Wannier

Louise Wannier is the founder and CEO of TRUUdesigns, a fashion design working studio and online resource for women of all ages. Her studio is a warm, light-filled, visually inspiring gathering place for cultural and social experiences that enhance the community. Louise founded MyShape to introduce "Me" Commerce – Personal Shopping online. She has founded and built five companies including prior consumer leadership success as co-founder and COO of Gemstar US and CEO of Gemstar Europe.

www.truudesigns.com

Jean Weidemann

Aligned with a Purpose

...First you begin to listen to messages from your heart — messages you may have ignored since childhood. Next you must take the daring step of expressing your heart to the outside world ...

~Martha Beck, American author

At the age of five, I looked at my mother and said, "When I grow up, I'm going to help the poor people in Africa." My mother is almost one hundred and still remembers the day I decided upon my life's work.

It wasn't until many years later that I found my way to Africa, and then it was almost by chance. I was working as a project leader in the United Nations Food and Agricultural Organization, and my husband was with a private international foundation. We wanted to work in the same country, but the only place in the world where we could get jobs together was in Nigeria.

My primary responsibility was helping women farmers who produced the bulk of the country's food supply. As the van approached a remote African village for my first meeting, I noticed that some women were pregnant, and they, like the others, carried older babies in wraps on their backs. Bent over under the scorching African sun, the women were working with the most prehistoric agricultural tools I had ever seen.

I was nervous wondering what they would think of a white American woman who, though she had grown up on a farm, could not really call herself a farmer the way these women could. When I exited the van, everyone dropped their tools and ran to welcome me with open arms. Then they began to sing and dance with joy! The Nigerian women were ecstatic to see me! Someone had come to help them!

Later, I listened in awe to their remarkable stories of strength and tenacity. The women explained that after working in the fields, they went home to take care of their children. On top of farming duties, they walked for miles to get firewood and clean water sometimes with only one meal and a small snack a day. They got pregnant often, but because of the lack of good medical care, some had lost more babies than they delivered.

In that moment I knew that I could not rest until I did something to make their lives better. What I didn't know was that I was on the ground floor of an unprecedented international movement, a project that would prove to be one of the first pioneering efforts to address gender inequality in the developing world.

That gender inequality was defined by the UN: Women are one-half of the world's people, who do two-thirds of the world's work, earn one-tenth of the world's income and own one-hundredth of the world's property. It was a long road ahead, but looking back, I feel great satisfaction knowing that many of the programs I helped to start during my almost four-decade career are still in place.

In spite of the trials and tribulations—long hours, grueling work, limited contact with the outside world, witnessing executions, riding in cars that were stoned, being robbed and contracting malaria —whenever I checked in with my heart, it said that I was aligned with my purpose and doing exactly what I was born to do.

~ Jean Weidemann

Jean Weidemann is founder and president of the Weidemann Foundation, a nonprofit organization emphasizing microlending and sustainable development to combat global poverty. Recognized worldwide as a microlending specialist, she authored over forty books and publications including "Supporting Women's Livelihoods: Microfinance that Works for the Majority". She worked for the UN, US State Department, and World Bank, among others, and is listed in Who's Who in America and Who's Who in the World.

www.createglobalchange.org

Lynda Weinman

A Definition of Success

*Success to me to not about money or status or fame; it's about finding
a livelihood that brings me joy and self-sufficiency and a sense of contributing to the world.*

~Anita Roddick, founder, Body Shop

My start with teaching people about computers and software grew
out of my own experience and frustrations. When I was twenty-
seven and working in animation, my boyfriend at the time bought a
computer, and like many people back then, I had no interest in
learning how to use one. He was so convinced that I should give it
a try, I did.

When I opened the manual, I was sure the instructions were
written to deliberately confuse a nontechnical person like me. I
managed to learn a few basic things, but every little victory was like
fighting an uphill battle. Once I was able to teach myself the basics,
I was able to use the computer to make my work easier.

Two years later, I purchased my own computer. The rapid changes in the world of technology in that short amount of time were fascinating. I was mesmerized by the icons and the ease of using a mouse to point to and move items on the screen. It made my work easier, and in less than a year, the skills I had built up as a hobby were in very high demand. But even as computers got a lot less difficult to use, manuals were just as impossible to understand and weren't written for actual humans to comprehend.

I thought my career would continue to be involved in animation and graphics using a computer as my tool. But I found my true skill to be my ability to explain computers and software in real language, for real people. I started a consulting practice, wrote magazines, spoke at conferences and taught classes at colleges and universities. I wrote the first book on web design because no other text books were available for my students. Suddenly I was helping people around the world—and I loved it.

The royalties from my first book enabled my family to move to a new home away from the city where our daughter could grow up in an idyllic country setting. Instead of having me travel all the time to teach, we opened a school and students came from around the globe to learn web design.

After the dot-com crash and 9/11, people had less expendable income for travel, so we adapted and launched our online learning library. Our company has grown beyond our wildest dreams! Today we have over 300 employees and more than 200 instructors reaching millions of people online, and every week we receive emails and letters from our members thanking us for our service.

One day I noticed that many of these emails are still addressed directly to me. These emails don't thank me for showing them how to mask in Photoshop or how to export a spreadsheet. People thank me for changing their lives and expanding their opportunities, like getting a new job or a raise, or giving them hope for a better future.

I realized that doing what I love brings tangible rewards as my company grows: new ways for students to learn and opportunities for our employees to buy new homes, send their children to excellent schools and invest in retirement accounts. In that moment I understood the truth of the saying, "Do what you love and the money will follow."

Sharing what I know and love every day changes lives for the better—for me and for millions of others. *This* is my definition of success.

~ Lynda Weinman

__Lynda Weinman__, a web graphics and design veteran, is cofounder and executive chair of lynda.com, an online learning company teaching software, creative, and business skills for personal and professional success. She wrote the first book on web design, <designing web graphics>. Lynda is a prominent educator and author of dozens of best-selling books, was a faculty member at Art Center College in Pasadena, and worked as an animator and motion graphics director in the film special effects industry.

www.lynda.com

Denita Willoughby

The Right Call

… Being open to unexpected twists in the road is an important part of success. If you try to plan every step, you may miss those wonderful twists and turns. Just find your next adventure, do it well, enjoy it, and then not now, think about what comes next.

~Condoleeza Rice

An important turning point in my life occurred during a conversation with two executives who reported to the chairman of the Fortune 500 Company where I had worked for fifteen years. We were discussing my future and how quickly I had progressed to the position of Vice President compared to my peer group.

The executives wanted to know what I had envisioned as the next step in my career. I said that my dream was to be an officer, a CEO, CFO or President of a business unit of the company by the time I was forty. Then they asked the question that changed everything—was I willing to relocate?

They explained that company policy dictated that senior level executives must gain broad exposure and visibility in different cities across different business lines. Some Vice Presidents move four or five times. Because California is one of the largest markets in the country, I had always thought that I might be able to make it all the way to officer without needing to relocate.

My husband had his own law firm, and my children were happy and doing well in school. The last thing I wanted as a wife and mother was to upset their lives. I either had to surrender my dream and settle for my career staying where it was or I had to do something I never thought I'd have to do: make a move outside the company. But I didn't want to leave! I had a great job! The company had groomed me and educated me, and I planned to retire there!

Looking at the executives, I said, "I'm sorry, but I am not mobile. I love working here, but my family comes first." At that moment I saw the writing on the wall, and it became crystal clear that my decision had eliminated any opportunity for future advancement. "It's your call," they said. "If you want to be promoted, you must be willing to relocate. We will not make you an officer in Los Angeles."

Walking away from a successful fifteen-year career was a very scary move for me. It was the biggest transition in my life! Looking back, I'm happy that I was grounded and clear about my priorities, and I'm proud that I had the courage to make the right call.

It is important for women to have solid guiding principles that will lead us down the path to success. For me, that means always putting my family first and staying focused on what makes me truly happy.

~ Denita Willoughby

Denita Willoughby is CEO of The Wiki Group, Inc. Previously she was with AT&T as Vice President of External Affairs in the Greater Los Angeles Area. Named by California Diversity Magazine as one of the Most Powerful and Influential Women in California, Denita has an engineering degree from the University of Wisconsin-Madison and an MBA from Harvard Business School. She is a member of the board for California Institute of the Arts, Green Dot Public Schools, Unite LA and Vision to Learn.

www.thewikigroup.com

Jane Wurwand

Speaking Up For Change

The global statistics on the abuse of girls are numbing. … We believe that in this century the paramount moral challenge will be the struggle for gender equality around the world.

~Sheryl WuDunn & Nicholas Kristof,
authors, *Half the Sky*

"Oh my God," I gasped reading *Half the Sky*. "I am so lucky to live in America where girls have the right to get an education and where women have unlimited opportunities to achieve financial independence. I am blessed as a mother of girls in a country where my two daughters can be loved and protected!"

My eyes were opened to the atrocities of the greatest humanitarian crisis of our time: the brutal oppression of women in developing countries. Hundreds of thousands of innocent young girls sold as sex slaves. Honor killings and mass rape. Forced prostitution, bride-burning, wife-beating and sexual-mutilation. Violence that claims the life of a woman every minute!

It was shocking to learn that in the twenty-first century, millions of girls "disappear" every year because of gender discrimination. In some places a baby is killed every four minutes because she committed the crime of being born a girl. The real-life stories of suffering endured by impoverished women were absolutely gut-wrenching.

I thought about my mother who was thirty-eight years old when my father, a major in the British Army, died of a heart attack. As was customary in England in 1944 my mother never expected to have a job outside the home after marriage. Suddenly responsible for raising four young daughters alone, paying a mortgage and putting food on the table, she was able to get a job and return to work as a nurse.

Even at the age of three, I knew my mother was a woman of incredible strength and courage. But what would have happened to my sisters and me if our mother had been born in a part of the world where she didn't have the ability to support her family?

After the loss of our father, my mother instilled the importance of choosing a career that would enable her daughters to be financially independent no matter where we went in the world. When it was time to choose my future life's work, I attended beauty school to learn a transportable skill in a rapidly growing industry dominated by women.

Moving to California with my boyfriend, whom I later married, I continued my career in the beauty business, and over time we became leaders in the professional skin care industry. My proudest accomplishment is the knowledge that Dermalogica has helped thousands of women to achieve financial security doing something they love. I wished that it was possible to help the unfortunate women in *Half the Sky*, but living on the other side of the planet, what could I do?

Then I thought, "Wait a minute! Didn't my mother prove that a woman can achieve the impossible if she has a skill? My company is all about women. My entire career has been devoted to helping women unleash the power of financial independence." I started to think that if these women had a way to support themselves and their families like my mother did in her time of crisis, miracles could happen.

Lending money to women in developing countries to start or grow a business produces a very high return on investment, yet statistics show that a bank is far more likely to give a loan to a man. Women and girls are not the problem. They are the solution! Why not use my experience as an entrepreneur to find a way to provide these women with opportunities for financial assistance so they could start their own businesses?

In that moment I literally heard the voices of the women and girls in *Half the Sky* call out to me. "Please speak up for us!" they cried in total despair. "Use your voice to help us! We need you!" The depths of their pain and misery broke my heart. "I am here for you," I promised, "and I will do everything in my power to help."

The realization that I could use my voice to speak up for change in the global fight for the betterment of women was life-changing. I can make a difference! So can you.

~ Jane Wurwand

Jane Wurwand is the founder of Dermalogica, the leading professional skin care company which has helped over 100,000 women worldwide to become successful entrepreneurs as skin care therapists and salon owners. Jane co-founded nonprofit joinFITE.org (Financial Independence Through Entrepreneurship) with Kiva.org to provide women in developing countries with access to small loans that will empower them to start or grow a sustainable business.

www.dermalogica.com

Laura Yamanaka

An Extraordinary Promise

Tell me, what is it you plan to do with your one wild and precious life?

~Mary Oliver, American poet

My life has been shaped by a woman I met only once at the age of seven—my tiny, courageous Japanese great-grandmother. She and my great-grandfather and their five children immigrated to Hawaii for better opportunities over one hundred years ago.

Sadly, my great-grandfather died very suddenly. My great-grandmother, a young widow in a new country with no family and no means of support, was left to raise five kids on her own. In order to take care of her children, she started a business making sandwiches for the Japanese field workers who came to Hawaii to earn a living.

My mother often told me stories about the difficult life my great-grandmother had led. In Japan, if you were a girl, you were treated like a second class citizen. Everything, and every opportunity, automatically went to the boys. As a result, she made a promise to all her five children: each one would learn a trade—especially the girls.

At that point in time, my great-grandmother's promise was extraordinary because in the Japanese culture it was unthinkable that any woman would make sure that her lowly daughters were taught how to support themselves. Since then, all the girls in my great-grandmother's line have been brought up to believe that it is our responsibility to find a career that will enable us to support ourselves in the manner in which we wish to live.

My great-grandmother's philosophy has held true for me, and I have passed it along to all my children. The concept of being able to support myself in the manner in which I wish to live has set the tone for many of the choices I have made and has empowered me to get to where I am today as the president of my own business.

I was coming out of the security of corporate America when I took the big leap into entrepreneurship. Having worked in large corporations for my entire life, I wanted to do something on my own. My great-grandmother's courage in starting her own business was the push I needed to create my own company. "Hey" I thought, "If I want to control my own destiny, then I need to be able to craft my own life. What am I waiting for?"

Until that moment I hadn't thought about my great-grandmother for quite a while. I was just a small seven-year-old child the only time we were together. Yet I vividly recalled towering above a tiny, bent-over elderly woman who snuck me pieces of candy by the cash register of a restaurant that was once a simple sandwich business.

She didn't speak English and I didn't speak Japanese, but I was absolutely fascinated by her. To me, she was the best thing in the whole world. I didn't understand that this tiny woman was the same person my mother had always talked about—my courageous Japanese great-grandmother whose extraordinary promise would shape my life.

~ Laura Yamanaka

Laura Yamanaka is the president and founder of team CFO that provides finance and accounting services to a broad spectrum of service and product-based industries. Laura was honored by the Small Business Administration as a Woman in Business Champion of the Year and also received the Wells Fargo Asian Business Leadership Award. She currently serves as national president of the National Association of Women Business Owners.

www.teamCFO.com

Mahvash Yazdi

Still In the Pursuit of Excellence

Ask yourself: Have you been kind today? Make kindness your daily modus operandi and change your world.
~Annie Lennox, Scottish singer &
songwriter

Sometimes people are surprised to know that before the 1979 Iranian Revolution, women held respected positions of leadership in a wide variety of professions. When I was growing up during the mid-1950s and 60s, the idea of a woman pursuing excellence was nothing out of the ordinary.

My parents' dream was for all seven of their children, five girls and two boys, to be highly educated. Wanting their daughters to have successful careers and to stand on their own two feet, my parents would say, "Don't get married so your husband can take care of you. Get married for love."

When I was a senior in high school, my family moved to California so my siblings and I could attend college in the United

States. I met my husband the first week of my freshman year. After earning our degrees in 1974, we married and returned to Iran which was growing quickly and had many opportunities for educated workers.

Very excited about working with computers, I accepted a job in Tehran with IBM. Within the first year, my superiors asked me to emcee the annual kickoff meeting attended by over four-hundred people. At the age of twenty three, this was truly an honor!

The theme of the day was "In Pursuit of Excellence." When the meeting began, we watched a video showing how a masterpiece is produced—a young conductor was preparing to lead the Los Angeles Philharmonic Orchestra in a rendition of "Bolero." Gradually, the conductor directed the musicians to increase the intensity of sounds and   skillfully invited the various instruments to join in. The crescendo at the end, with all the musicians playing in perfect harmony, took my breath away.

I was struck by the realization that, although each musician had undoubtedly worked very hard to master his instrument, the conductor's vision was what had created the magic. "Professional excellence," I thought, "means having a vision. It's about creating and motivating a great team and making sure everyone performs at their best level." Deeply inspired, in that moment I decided to create a habit of excellence for myself.

A few years later, oppressive political changes began to sweep through Iran. My husband and I decided to leave everything we owned and take our young children back to the United States. As we struggled to rebuild our lives, I learned that excellence is not only a habit—it is very much a state of mind. Again, I had to create a vision for my life: What did I want to do? Where did I want to go? What sacrifices was I willing to make?

I thought about "Bolero" and how it must have taken years of practice for each musician to perfect their portion of a masterpiece.

In this country, anything is possible if you put your mind to it. I came from a foreign country under difficult circumstances, yet I worked my way up to the executive level. In America, every woman is blessed with the opportunity to be the conductor of her own life.

Recently, I celebrated a milestone birthday. Reflecting upon the six decades of my life, I thought about the many acts of kindness that have been extended to me and my family. Some were great efforts and others were simple acts that lifted my soul as I struggled through life's challenges. So, instead of a large celebration, I composed a list of "60 Acts of Kindness" and shared it with my family, friends and coworkers.

Some of my acts have already been completed; some are still in progress. I could never have imagined how much positive energy and good will my list would generate! I have come to realize that excellence is never achieved in one single event, but rather through the consistent and steadfast pursuit of those things that we believe to be of great value.

I'd like to share a special goal on my list of "60 Acts of Kindness" — "To unite the Iranian American community and have its voice heard. To celebrate who we are and pass our heritage to future generations. To give back to America as it has given to us."

~ Mahvash Yazdi

Mahvash Yazdi is the Senior Vice President for Information Technology and Business Integration and Chief Information Officer at Southern California Edison. Under her leadership, SCE's Information Technology organization is recognized as one of the best 100 places to work. A member of the Trusteeship of the International Women's Forum, she is a recipient of the Ellis Island Medal of Honor awarded to American citizens who exemplify outstanding community service and celebrate the traditions of their ancestry.

Afterword

The conclusion of our conversations with the 108 amazing women featured in this book was a bittersweet moment. We almost didn't want the exhilarating journey to end!

Here are some lessons we learned along the way:

- In order to get anything in life, you must believe in yourself. Nothing is impossible if you set your sights high and refuse to give up. Don't let "your fear getcha!"

- Be aligned with your purpose. Excellence means having a vision. If you don't like the direction your life is taking, switch gears and do something else.

- You are never too young or too old to better the world. Do something positive with your life … *now.*

- Don't be afraid of criticism; do what you love. Take big "calculated" risks. Have the courage to say "yes" when a moment of opportunity comes your way.

- Claim your destiny! There are many different ways to serve the world. Find work that speaks to your heart. Be brave. You can do it. Just take it day by day.

- With a positive attitude, we can transcend adversity, be transformed by it and go on to prosper and thrive. We are so much stronger than we know.

- Time is measured by heart beats and moments. Make every moment in your life count!

Love,

Patty & Maureen

P.S. We hope you will spread the word about *Life Moment for Women* to everyone you know. Please become our partners in the quest to raise $1,000,000 for the Women's Foundation of California.

Patty DeDominic

Entrepreneur, strategic adviser, supporter of women's issues, Patty DeDominic is a force of nature. In 1979 she founded PDQ Personnel Services, Inc., and later acquired CT Engineering, that grew into a powerhouse staffing agency. In 2006, she sold her businesses to a privately held firm that is now over one billion dollars in annual sales nationally and one of the nation's largest human resources and staffing firms.

Patty was named Chief Executive Officer of the Year by the LA Business Journal and has received over twenty distinguished awards including recognition by the United States Department of Labor and other organizations as one of America's finest employers; The Bank One Top Customer Service Award; The Artemis Award presented in Greece; and The President's Award from Women Impacting Public Policy (WIPP) presented in Washington, DC. She was inducted into the Women's Business Owners Hall of Fame over ten years ago.

The non-profit world has been Patty's special passion, and for over 20 years she has been a board member in the National Association of Women Business Owners and Chambers of Commerce, SCORE and leading non-profit organizations like the Jane Goodall Institute and Direct Relief International. In 2007 she launched the International Women's Festivals to celebrate women around the world in conjunction with International Women's Day.

Capitalizing on over two decades of successful experiences as an entrepreneur and board member, she currently operates DeDominic & Associates, a specialized business consulting firm that offers professional services to enterprise builders www.dedominic.com

Other books by Patty include *Land It, Job Hunting Tips for Prime of Lifers* and *Get It, Shortcuts to Job Success* (for new grads).

Patty and her husband, Gene Sinser, live in Santa Barbara. They raised five children and have five grandchildren.

Maureen E. Ford

Maureen Ford's greatest passion has always been teaching, working with young people and helping students to accomplish their dreams.

So it is no surprise that after graduating from St. John's University in New York with a degree in Education, Maureen focused her career in the non-profit sector where she believed her professional efforts could make the greatest difference.

In 1987 she started the Southern California Entrepreneurship Academy, an innovative educational program for college students who aspired to start a business. As personal advisor and mentor to hundreds of students and start-up companies in Southern California, she received the prestigious Entrepreneur of the Year Award from Ernst & Young and the Orange County business community.

Prior to building SCEA, Maureen was a high school teacher and later worked for the March of Dimes Birth Defects Foundation where she developed and delivered training programs and workshops around the country to benefit the health and lives of our nation's women and children.

Believing in the importance of giving back, Maureen has had an impressive record of volunteer work, public service and leadership roles in local city government committees and emergency response teams. She has been an active member in philanthropic organizations focused on needs for women and girls, such as the Palos Verdes Juniors Women's Club, Sandpipers of the South Bay and organizations that assist victims of sexual abuse and domestic violence.

Life Moments for Women is the culmination of Maureen's passion for mentoring, a wonderful gift that truly keeps on giving. She resides in Rancho Palos Verdes with her high school sweetheart and husband, Patrick J. Ford.

Acknowledgements

Life Moments for Women would not have been possible without the support and collaboration of many dedicated people who truly care about the well-being and advancement of California's women and girls.

Deepest appreciation to our sponsors: Denita Willoughby, AT&T, Boehm Gladen Foundation and New York Life.

Special thanks to:

Cathy Feldman, Blue Point Books, publisher/book designer extraordinaire, whose patience and professional guidance kept us on track and brought everything together;

Carol Holdsworth, Three-Sixty Marketing & Communications, who magically appeared in our lives at the perfect moment;

Additional thanks to: our photographer, Deb Halberstadt, Half City Productions, Matt LaBland, DeDominic & Associates, Kim Kenny, Women's Foundation of California, The Willoughby Group, Anita D'Aquilar and UBS, as well as our friends at the Central Coast office of New York Life, Jane Choi, Del Hegland and Brad Johnson.

We can never forget the amazing contributions of Patrick Ford and Gene Sinser, our husbands, best friends and soul mates, who supported our dream every step of the way. Patrick and Gene, thank you!

And, of course, we are forever indebted to the amazing 108 women who have generously given their time and opened their hearts to us and everyone who reads this book.

About the Women's Foundation of California

The Women's Foundation of California is a publicly supported grant-making foundation that invests in women as a key strategy for creating a California where all communities are economically secure and can thrive. Since 1979, the Foundation has cultivated diverse cross community relationships by making grants to effective organizations, training nonprofit leaders and bringing the voices of women into public policymaking. For more information visit

www.womensfoundca.org
